The ThinkNP Guide to Nonprofit Consulting

A Practical Workbook for Your Success

Matthew A. Hugg

Sunnybrae Press

ISBN-13: 978-0-9892571-1-4

TO MICHAEL

Only see the possibilities in front of you.

CONTENTS

ACKNOWLEDGMENTS

Thanks much to Jason Hugg (www.huggmedia.com)

and Carol Hugg for their untiring support on this project.

Special thanks also to John Burns, of John Burns Design Group
(www.johnburnsdesigngroup.com) for his fine work on the ThinkNP logo.

PREFACE

Preparing for consulting.

This guidebook takes you through the steps to get you ready for nonprofit consulting. Whether you're exploring, starting up, or an experienced consultant, you'll find powerful exercises to build your confidence, identify where you need to grow, and set a platform for hitting the ground running in your new consulting business.

To get the most out of this book, "The ThinkNP Guide to Nonprofit Consulting: A Practical Workbook for Your Success," pair it with a membership to ThinkNP.com. While these pages and ThinkNP both give you the basics, you'll come to rely on ThinkNP as your continuing education program for nonprofit consulting success.

One more thing, a disclaimer… This book is based on my experience and represents my opinions. In it, I also provide references to websites and books whose thoughts and opinions are their own, not mine. In the end, it is up to you to engage professional advice on the topics presented. I am not responsible for your success: you are! So go get that success!

Best wishes… Matt

1 INTRODUCTION

Ready to start?

Consulting for nonprofits is great. At least I've found it that way. I trust that you will, too.

I opened my business as a consultant to nonprofits more than 10 years ago, before the Great Recession. I stayed in business during the meltdown and after, and remain so today. Was it frustrating at times? Sure. Was there stress and anxiety? Yup. Did I say some days "time to get a job!" Once or twice. Could it all go away tomorrow? You bet. Would I trade it for anything else? Never!

Over the years my business has evolved. It started from a general consulting firm to doing what I found I enjoyed, and others told me I did best: writing and teaching.

I started with a solid foundation in my discipline: fundraising for nonprofits. I have one of the first master's degrees in the field, and had a fine track record of building development offices and raising money. Like a lot of you, I had the "skills" box checked, rechecked and checked again.

What I didn't have was any marks in the "business" checkbox.

I did a lot of research to start, and made my share of mistakes. What I've found over the years was that my start was pretty typical. Nearly everyone I met knew how to do their core business. Few, at least among the independent consultants, started with a grasp of what it took to start and run their business... and they suffered greatly for it. Many stopped consulting because of it.

That's why you have this book. It's also why you have the videos, podcasts and articles found at ThinkNP.com: so you can get a running start to creating a successful nonprofit consulting business.

Your success in building a business, consulting practice, freelancing career or whatever you plan to call what you're doing, is going to depend a lot on how you use your time. To help put you, and keep you on the right track, always keep three numbers in mind: 60, 30 and 10.[1]

- Sixty percent of your time needs to be in marketing and sales. You can't do anything unless someone agrees to pay you to do whatever it is that you do. To keep those jobs coming in consistently, you have to keep up your marketing.

- Thirty percent of your time should be devoted to doing the greatest job of whatever it is you do. Whether its running the best fundraising campaign, designing the greatest brochures, accounting for every penny your nonprofit client spends, that's what they're paying you for, so give them the best.

- Ten percent is what I call "infrastructure" (your "back office") That's creating the contracts and getting out the bills, putting out the trash and cleaning your desk, organizing your computer files and updating your database. Infrastructure is the background work that keeps the marketing and client work humming.

This book, and ThinkNP.com, is about the 60+10: the 70 percent of what makes a business thrive. Most people come to nonprofit consulting as solid 30 percent folks. They know their field inside and out. Unfortunately, that's not enough. You need to be super at the 70 percent. That's how people know you're great at the 30 percent.

Early in my career, a lot of my family and friends looked at me quizzically when I said I was going to work at a nonprofit. "Nonprofit means they don't have money, right?" Well, no. It means they don't distribute profits to shareholders, among other attributes. You and I know that healthy nonprofit runs balanced budgets, if not surpluses, which they plow back into their missions.

(Today when someone says to me "nonprofits have no money," I just smile. Why? If someone wants to cut themselves out of a good market, no problem. I'll be there making money.)

Consulting for nonprofits is kind of an "odd duck" sort of business. It has a lot of attributes that make it just like consulting for another business. Yet nonprofits are not businesses, just like government is not a business. That distinction means you can't approach them as businesses. Like any good sales person, you need to meet your customer where they are, not how you see them. I like to call it "B2N."

(¹ I first found this concept in Jeffrey J. Fox's "How to make big money in your own small business: unexpected rules every small business owner needs to know," (Jeffrey J Fox 2004 Hyperion, New York, New York) but have since seen it in several other sources.)

Defining B2N

When I say "business-to-business," chances are you know what I mean. In case you don't (and there's no shame in a bit of education), it's when you, a business, sell your services to another business. In contrast, there's "business to consumer," where you sell your services to an end-user. For example, a retail business is a "business to consumer" enterprise. "Business to consumer" is often called "B2C" and "business to business" is known as "B2B."

Are you a B2B business? You're selling your services to another organizational entity, in effect, a business, right? Still, there's something not quite the same. Yes, you're selling to a "business," but a nonprofit is not a typical business organization. It's a nonprofit, which often looks like a business from the outside, has many of the same functions as a business on the inside, but whose mission and purpose is very different than the local drugstore down the street, or accounting firm next door.

That's why I think it's important to come up with a new identity for what we do: "B2N." B2N, or "business-to-nonprofit" better describes what we do because our clients don't behave in ways that are typical of most businesses. They have a "double bottom line." On one hand, they have to balance their books. At least breaking even or showing a profit, or as it's known in the nonprofit world, a surplus, is essential for financial viability. That's not too much different than a business.

However, it's that second bottom line, the mission, which turns everything on its head. An organization's mission will even affect its other bottom line, its finances. What may seem like a decision to question in a business might be perfectly rational in a nonprofit. For example, how many of us would willingly lose money when servicing our customers? Yet that's what happens every day in the nonprofit sector, because the customers are the clients and the clients are the purpose of their mission.

To understand this, it's important to "follow the money." In a business, if you have a product to sell, and if your client wants your product, you give the product to the client and the client gives you money. Transaction done. It is a bilateral relationship.

In a nonprofit, this becomes more complicated. You have a mission. Your mission is to provide a service. You give that service either free of charge or at a reduced price to your mission recipient. Then you turn to your donor and say "can you pay for that?" It is this trilateral relationship that makes nonprofits unique. It's that focus on mission that makes everything else happen.

Of course, not all nonprofits raise money through charitable gifts. Many get their revenue exclusively from government grants or insurance companies, and others operate similar to businesses, using a fee-for-service model.

Regardless of the revenue source, what remains the same in any nonprofit is a dedication to mission over profits. That's why it's important for us to reconsider "B2B," and think of our relationship as "B2N."

So, if you're in B2N, then chances are you're not dealing with a client's business culture, but their nonprofit culture.

The Nonprofit Culture

Years ago, when I worked for a university that had a very strong arts program, once in a while I would run into students who would say something to the effect of "I want to do my work nonprofit."

I had to think for a bit on what they meant. When I asked, I found out that they saw nonprofits as the "anti-business." Their assumption was that the business environment was toxic and working in a nonprofit culture was much more conducive to their life goals. For some who were considering starting their own organization, the nonprofit moniker felt friendlier and more democratic.

Much of what these students attributed to nonprofits is true, and a lot of it was mythology.

Fundamentally, a human organization is a human organization, whether it's a business, nonprofit, government or other structure. The culture is determined by who started it and who has carried on the organization's legacy. Whether that organization is a nonprofit, a business, or a government entity does not really bear on many of its cultural attributes. Through my life I have run into very "touchy-feely" businesses and many button-down, corporate feeling nonprofits.

Still, the nature of a nonprofit will have some impact on an organization's culture. Being mission driven is core to any nonprofit and attracts many who apply for employment, and therefore how its culture develops. Below you'll find a list of "typical" characteristics of many nonprofit organizations. Of course, few nonprofits have all of these attributes, and many have none of them. If using these as a guide, keep this in mind.

(Many of these are culled from Teegarden, Hinden and Sturm's "The Nonprofit Organizational Culture Guide: Revealing the Hidden Truths that Impact Performance" and others are based on my own experience.)

Cultural characteristics
- Mission focused.
- Passionate.
- Resource constrained.
- Success equals mission; success does not equal money.
- Process oriented.
- Consensus driven, flat, not pyramid in structure.
- Slow (deliberate?) decision-making: frustration.
- Money is a means in a nonprofit, not an end.
- "Feel" or act poor vs. your "big business," regardless that your business is just you
- Nonprofits are more vulnerable to negative press. Scrutiny is intense when things go wrong.

Embezzlement at a business rarely hits the news, but at a nonprofit, it's front-page.
- Like anyone, they don't like to be labeled as "do-gooders" or foolish. They're serious about what they do, even though it may seem "frivolous" to someone else.

Nonprofit staffing
- Passionate about the cause.
- Some have a lifelong interest in their passion.
- May have personal connection to their cause.
- Firing is more of an emotional experience in a nonprofit because a staff person's passion for the cause.
- Nonprofits can operate fiefdoms.
- Nonprofit leadership is usually experts at the nonprofit's core mission, but they are often not educated as professional managers.
- Some nonprofit workers went into their work as the "anti-business."
- They see their nonprofit as part of a distinctive community focused on their mission.
- The nonprofit workers can have a love/hate relationship with money.
- More women work at nonprofits, but there is an ongoing issue that the men get paid higher. (https://trust.guidestar.org/blog/2015/11/20/women-in-nonprofits-then-now/)

Nonprofit business operations
- Flexible work conditions and environments.
- Few "standard" approaches.
- Nonprofits have own infrastructure systems. Be careful when imposing a "business solution" label to a process.
- They see you as either wanting money and not committed to the mission, or as an overhead expense.
- Don't understand why you can't give your services to them for free.
- Extremely cost conscious.
- Often dependent on government support.
- Penny wise/pound foolish.
- Nonprofits are risk averse. Although they may have the same revenue and number of employees than a comparable business, I've found that more nonprofits are led by managers who "work for an organization" and therefore are more risk averse. This contrasts with small businesses who tend to be led by entrepreneurs and "work for themselves." The small business leaders tend to make their decisions with more independence than their nonprofit counterpart. Of course, these are generalizations. Your experience will vary.

Nonprofit work environment
- Makes up for what they think is poor pay by offering flexible hours.
- Relaxed dress codes.
- Take a social justice stance on some issue and not others, and seem inconsistent (like pay).

- Non-mission activities less valued – even if income generating or saving.
- Frustration with length of decision making process.
- One person wears many, many hats.

Nonprofit founders:
- Not too much different than business founder.
- May have personal interest in cause.
- Have a tough time seeing anything other than their personal vision.
- Board maybe "friends and family" and therefore not effective.
- Have no financial incentive to merge with similar organizations.
- Have hard time loosening grip.
- Can put vision over practical considerations.
- Can see others as "not dedicated enough."
- Use the nonprofit they started as therapy for issues that drive them.
- Suffer from "founder syndrome."

Nonprofit Boards
- Every nonprofit has to have a board of directors, also known as "trustees."
- Many, if not all board members are non-experts in the mission of the nonprofit.
- Generally, the smaller the nonprofit, the more influence the board has in financial decision making.
- Boards have more influence in nonprofits than in for-profits.
- There are worker boards, and policy boards.
- Many boards are protected from staff. This isolates them from politics, and also reality
- Could be friends and family, political, community, client program, or power boards
- All board members should be donors.
- Boards frequently interfere with staff work.
- Boards are legal stewards, but often do not take the responsibility seriously.
- Working with a board can be very political.

Exercise 1

Name at least five characteristics from the list above have you seen in either a former workplace, client or volunteer experience.

_____

_____

_____

_____

_____

_____

Exercise 2

Consider how your experiences can…

Add up to a bias against nonprofit culture.

_____

_____

_____

Aid you in relating to nonprofit clients.

_____

_____

_____

Are you ready to be a nonprofit consultant?

Here's a list of signs that could indicate that your "inner consultant" is ready to get out.

- Do you feel like you are an expert in a skill or service that many organizations could benefit from?
- Are you interested in a variety of missions, or how a number of organizations express similar missions?
- Do you like teaching?
- Do you see solutions to problems that other people don't even know they have?
- Are you anxious to apply your skills to new places?
- Is "telecommuting" and "flextime" not in your employer's lexicon?
- Did someone in your family, or a personal role model, have his or her own business?
- Does the word "boss" make you chafe?
- Are you making valuable contributions without the recognition you think you deserve?
- Do you like working in different environments?
- Do you have personal discipline to accomplish projects with no supervision?

Exercise 3

How many of the above attributes do you have? ____

Circle them.

Why you DON'T want to be a consultant!

You might think this is an odd statement in a book that is generally encouraging about consulting, freelancing or being a vendor to nonprofits. In fact, it's a great life. Yet if you don't look, even for a moment, at what can either go wrong or what you might not like, you will be all the more discouraged when you encounter it for yourself. So here we go:

Money. We'll just start straight off with what many consider the biggest issue.

- No regular paycheck. This is a given. Unless you set up a series of retainer clients, which is highly unlikely to start, your income will vary considerably through the year. After the first year or two you'll get used to it and be able to plan around it - saving sometimes for the lean times, and knowing when you'll be able to take some scheduled time, or not scheduled time off.

- Probably not "big bucks" especially at start. I would love to tell you that this is not true. The problem is a lot of your clients are certain that you're making all sorts of money off of them. We'll get into that later, but know that starting your consulting with personal reserves is, if not essential, a real help. Underfunding is one of the major causes of business failure.

- Most of your clients will be making more than you. Again, at least the start, you will be the poor person around the table. With diligence that will change, but know that at the start, even poor nonprofit staff's salaries will be greater than yours, to start. Try not to be envious.

- Healthcare. Regardless of where you are in the political spectrum, chances are you think that the American healthcare system is messed up. You're probably right. For the micro-business person, you have a couple of options. If you are coming to consulting after being laid off from a job where you had healthcare, you might be offered to pay into their healthcare via COBRA, at least for a while. If you have a spouse who holds health insurance, your best option may be to buy into that program. If not, investigate your options via the Affordable Care Act (ACA) or its successor(s). Don't forget to check with your local Chamber of Commerce, too. Many chambers offer health plans for members that are reasonably affordable.

- Taxes. Quarterlies. Record keeping. As Ben Franklin reminded us, taxes will always be with us. As an independent business person, even if you are not engaged full-time, you may be obligated to pay your state, local municipality and federal government on a quarterly basis. Make sure that you keep careful records so that you're able to do this. It's also good to consult an accountant on this process.

- Deadbeat clients. Not everybody pays on time, and not everybody pays. One of the biggest issues that anyone in independent business faces are deadbeat clients. You can try to avoid this by choosing your clients carefully. Sometimes that works. Other times, regardless of your diligence, circumstances come up with a client that means you may never see a check for your work. Your remedy? You can file a legal claim, or, since you're working with a nonprofit, you just consider your work "volunteering," and never volunteer for them again.

Work

- Difficult work? Maybe. Depending on what your experiences were before you decide to become a consultant to nonprofits, hard work could be very familiar to you. I know someone who says "I came into this as a charitable gift fundraiser. I worked 80 hour weeks and barely saw my family. Being a consultant is a breeze!" Not everybody will have that experience. Just don't think when you hear that being in one's own business is hard, that they're overstating it. They're not. It is.

- Uncomfortable work? Certainly. There's one thing for certain, whatever business you choose to be in, you will not be comfortable with 100% of what you need to do. You might love the "core" of your business – the thing you do. What you might really not like is, for example, marketing, or accounting, or going to client meetings, or any of a dozen other things which grate against your personality, or you simply never did well. You have two choices. Get good enough in that aspect of whatever it is you are not now proficient in, so that you can at least either reasonably survive it, or outsource that deficiency to somebody who is great at it, and makes you look good and feel better about that part of your business. Either way, there are some things that just have to get done.

- Inconvenient hours. By their nature, many nonprofits put in long, inconvenient hours. People's problems can't be solved from 9 AM to 5 PM, Monday through Friday, and most board members are volunteers who can come to you after their work hours. So if you are consulting or otherwise working with a nonprofit, you need to be available when they are doing their work, not just when it is convenient for you.

- Discipline of work. Remember those job advertisements that said "candidate must be a self-starter?" You now have the job. You have no choice but to self-start, or fail.

- Vacation? Ironically, people who consult, a job that seems to have the most flexibility, seem to have the most difficult time taking time for themselves.

Culture.

- Isolation. While you may do pretty well alone, as humans, we're social beings, and the documented effects of solitary confinement are gruesome. Among our strongest human traits is to define who we are through our associations with others. This also means that we define who we are by who we exclude from our group. There's nothing necessarily wrong with this, we just need to understand it, and not be too surprised that by declaring ourselves a consultant, vendor, or freelancer, we find ourselves outside the group that we identified with for much of our professional life: nonprofit professionals.

- How others see you socially. There will be an adjustment period by others to your newly declared status. If you're not out the door by 8 AM, your neighbors think you don't work (anyone ask you to watch their children while they go to an appointment?), your hairdresser or barber thinks you've retired (as I found out when I took advantage of off-hour haircuts) and your friendly letter carrier thinks you're permanently unemployed (apparently he asked my neighbor). Some family members were concerned for me, and others were jealous.

- How others see you professionally. More than one former nonprofit colleagues thought that by calling myself a "consultant," I was simply putting a better sounding label on what they thought would be temporary unemployment. Worse yet, once I declared myself a consultant, a lot of colleagues cast me out of the nonprofit club. That came with assumptions – on behavior, attitude, actions, and much more. "Those consultants" are not like "us," because you know that they all do those "things," right? Well, probably not. To any of us, we make our lives easier if we can classify something and justify ourselves for doing it. It is the seeds of prejudice. I confess being surprised (and not nearly so analytical and thoughtful about it) when I encountered this attitude.

Exercise 4

Take the following list and put it in your order of concern, with 1 as the area that most concerns you. If you think of areas of concern that are specific to you, or that we missed, add them below in "Other."

____ No regular paycheck.
____ Probably not "big bucks" especially at start.
____ Most of your clients will be making more than you.
____ Healthcare.
____ Taxes.
____ Deadbeat clients.
____ Hard Work.
____ Uncomfortable work.
____ Inconvenient hours.
____ Discipline of work.
____ Vacation.
____ Isolation.
____ How others see you socially.
____ How others see you professionally.
____ Other (1) _____
____ Other (2) _____
____ Other (3) _____

The above is by no means an exhaustive list. It just gives you a flavor of some of what you're facing. If after reading this you decide to walk away, nobody would blame you. If you simply say "okay" and press on, that's great. If it motivates you, all the better!

In the end, the odds are against you. By year five, 50% of all businesses fail. (https://www.linkedin.com/pulse/20140915223641-170128193-what-are-the-real-small-business-survival-rates) Some are underfunded. Some owners don't like what they started. Some find there's no market for their product. The list goes on. Will that be you? Maybe. The good news is that you can increase your odds. How?

- **Preparation**. Preparation is key. As you'll see elsewhere in this book, we are talking about business preparation and personal preparation. You need to be emotionally ready for your business as much as professionally organized to carry it out.

- **Marketing**. In my opinion, too many consultants simply do not market themselves either enough, in the right ways, or at all. As we'll talk about elsewhere, people like to do "what they do," their specialty. Attracting clients so they can carry out their specialty is inconvenient, scary, boring...

- **"Grit."** A lot has been written about "grit" lately (see "Grit: The Power of Passion and Perseverance" by Angela Duckworth). It's a real thing. I can cite circumstances where someone has the business equivalent of a hangnail and gives up, and others who suffer indignities that would wear down the most stalwart, yet persevere.

- **And more than a bit of luck.** Luck is grossly underrated. It starts at birth and continues throughout life. In Texas right now, there's a housing products company retired regional manager who is a descendant of the Washington family.

(See: http://www.newsweek.com/americas-lost-monarchy-man-who-would-be-king-92243)

If he was lucky, Washington would have accepted the offer to be King of the United States, this man would have been his successor. King or corporate manager? A matter of luck. Can you "make your luck?" Maybe. You can certainly position yourself so that when luck occurs, you can take advantage of it. You can also decide that when luck runs against you, to not be defeated by it. Either way, many (most?) circumstances you cannot control. You can just try to be ready.

If anything above scares you away - no worries. Best to find out now than after investing a lot of hard work, money and reputation into a challenge you didn't welcome or wasn't ready for. If that's you, stop reading here. For everyone else, let's go! You can do this!

A brief story:

My first professional association meeting after I started consulting was an eye opener. I knew quite a few people there. I was excited to tell my friends that I was "on my own." The news seemed pretty well received.

While I was talking to people, I came upon a handful of folks that I didn't know. I was new at this "networking for business" thing, and I didn't get their business cards. "No worries," I thought to myself. I can get their names at the registration desk on my way out.

The event ended and when I passed by the registration table, I remembered to ask to see the list of attendees. "Oh, no," the woman behind the desk said with a suspicious tone. "You're a consultant, and I'm not allowed to give you the list."

Whoa! No? Wait. My mind was racing. "I pay the same dues, and last week, you would have let me walk away with the whole list!" It was clear that she had her orders. I left empty-handed.

Yes, don't be surprised if you run into this prejudice among nonprofit workers about "consultants." (And yes, even if the day before you were happily (or not) drawing a nonprofit paycheck.) By declaring yourself a for-profit business, you have removed yourself from the nonprofit clan. You might not have realized it, but they did.

How is the nonprofit clan defined? At the risk of over-generalizing (yes another stereotype), a lot of nonprofit workers see themselves "virtuous." They're dedicated to their organization's mission and the public good.

You, on the other hand, are not. As someone "in business," you're dedicated to your profit. To them, it's that simple.

While the line between the two may seem bright, what's going on in each other's heads is not.

- You're thinking: "At least you get a regular paycheck"

They're thinking: "I'll bet you make a lot of money!"

- You're thinking: "Must be nice to get a paid vacation."

They're thinking: "You get to leave here whenever you want."

- You're thinking: "They can't be working as hard as me!"

They're thinking: "They can't be working as hard as me!"

Like a lot of prejudice, there's not much grounding in it. However, that doesn't mean you don't have to deal with it.

Of course, there's the other side of this. I know that by defining ourselves as "business people" who serve the nonprofit sector, we make assumptions (based on our omniscient, global "experience" with "those nonprofit types") about our clients. It's unavoidable.

What to do? Know about it. Don't blithely walk into a situation where, as "the consultant" you say something that magnifies what poor assumptions that they (or you) already have.

For example, you might not think that at a down moment during a presentation, sharing your excitement about a dreamed-for vacation to Disney would be an issue. You know that you saved for it for years, and you're using the air miles you earned when you had a paycheck job.

Yet what seemed like innocent banter might simply reinforce a hard-to-shake stereotype.

When the feeling over-worked, feeling underpaid nonprofit worker looks at your proposal, they'll think that you and Mickey are taking food out of their client's mouths, and that could cost you a major project.

Why nonprofit consulting?

My friends and colleagues came to consulting, freelancing or as a vendor to nonprofits for all sorts of reasons.

They were fired from their regular job. Some couldn't find a job they liked, or one at all. Many were bored, or had a conflict with their employer? A lot were tired of office politics. A few had a change in family situation, whether children, spouse or parent. I've met a "trailing spouse" who just moved to a new city. I know the "semi-retired." Although nobody's admitted they couldn't resist the idea of a dream lifestyle of sleeping until 10 AM and working in their PJs and slippers, I'm sure there were a few. Others say they needed extra income and didn't want to flip burgers. So many more just wanted to be their own boss.

Regardless of why they pursued the work, most consultants to nonprofits that I know came from the nonprofit sector. The majority transitioned from a nonprofit "paycheck job" to consulting in the same field. For example, they were a development officer in a nonprofit, and now they consult on fundraising campaigns. A smaller number left their nonprofit work to take a job with a business that supports nonprofits, like selling for a company that creates plaques and recognition systems for fundraising campaigns. Each option put their nonprofit skills and connections to use for the nonprofit sector. They have an advantage as a former "insider."

Another, smaller group, approached the sector from the outside, through a more universal skill set. For example, a designer might typically develop brochures for businesses. He was recommended to a hospital by a board member. Others with more universal skills used by all sectors - business, government and nonprofit - include computer technicians, printers, financial experts, building maintenance companies and many, many more. They don't see any difference - a computer is a computer whether it's at a shelter or a hardware store. Among them, a special few will enjoy the nonprofit environment or connect with a cause. They'll seek more nonprofit clients, and begin to focus on the market.

Exercise 5

Take a couple of minutes to write down your path to consulting. Was it similar to any of the above, a combination of a few, or something completely different?

_____

_____

_____

Whatever way you come to working with nonprofits, it is important to answer this question:

What do you want out of nonprofit consulting?

It might surprise you to hear that a lot of people don't say "a paycheck" first.

While making a living, supplementing your income or whatever else you'd like to do with your earnings is important, for many, consulting is a lifestyle decision. Sorry, walking barefoot on the beach while you're advising a client over the phone on their next gala probably won't happen. I mean, who could hear you with the waves crashing in the background? Then, why would you even take the call? You're on vacation!

Besides, that's not what I mean about "lifestyle." Really, what most people mean is flexibility; and related, what some would call "work/life balance." Whether that's making time around other family member's schedules - spouse, child, parent - or deciding that you're going to make every one of your child's sports events, you get to make that decision, not your boss. (Unless you have a client deadline…. hmmmm.) It could also be as simple as you're just not a "morning person." (I know one consultant who won't take client calls before 10 AM, but he works well into the night.)

The flip side of "flexibility" is discipline. "Discipline" not as in "punishment" (although for you, maybe it is?), but "discipline" as in the fortitude to put off the immediate gratification of playing a videogame or talking with friends on the phone, and focusing on the client's project to meet a deadline.

How about your environment? While you could work at your mountaintop retreat, you'll probably (at least to start) work at your dining room/now office, or your spare bedroom. You could also head to a nearby coffee shop. More on this, later.

I know people who consult because they relish the independence, and with that, the freedom from office politics. Being one's own boss is a very attractive proposition. It's also a bit illusionary. It's important to realize that as a consultant, you've traded one boss for many bosses, otherwise known as "clients." For some, there's security in this. At your paycheck job, if your boss wakes up grumpy and you make an ill-considered remark, you could come home without a job. As a consultant, if you have ten clients and one's grumpy, you have nine more clients. And you can pick those ten. Nobody's forcing you to take a client you don't like, unlike working with the office pariah when your boss thinks you deserve it.

Consulting is also a great learning experience. In nonprofit consulting you meet a wide variety of people, and work in environments you may never otherwise see. You may also find that when people feel comfortable with your skills, and enjoy working with you, you'll get asked to do projects that you never had in mind. Why? Because hiring someone they like and trust, to them, is much better than going through the pain and risk of finding someone new.

And as for money? Believe it or not, you decide what you make. Yes, you heard that right. You set your rates. You get the clients to fill your schedule. You decide how many hours you're working. Sounds easy, right? Not at all… otherwise you won't be reading this book!

Review the above section. What are the top three reasons (or more, if you want) you became a consultant? Share these with someone close to you. What's their reaction?

Exercise 6

Top reasons I want to become a consultant, and my close friend's response:
Reason   Response

_____

_____

_____

_____

_____

Who is a consultant?

For a few minutes, let's explore who calls themselves "consultants." It's a pretty wide range.

One of the nice things about consulting is its flexibility. Consulting is more than a job. It's a lifestyle. However, the word "consultant" describes an effort that is so broad that it is nearly meaningless to those people who are not engaged in the work. Let's look at the different ways you can be a consultant, not by skill set, but simply by how much time you do your work.

At one end of the spectrum, it's people who are in the full-time consulting business indefinitely. Some start right away as full-time, some gradually get there, and still others aspire to it.
Maybe you've jumped into this work fully and are plying your trade for many hours (okay, probably more) as you would a full-time "paycheck job." This would apply to anybody who is a sole practitioner, or to others who work in bigger firms as one consultant among many.

Right along with them are full-time consultants who are really in transition between jobs. They're consulting for the income until they find another job, to keep their skills sharp in the transition, or to be able to say that they so something instead of (the socially deadly) "I'm unemployed." In between clients they look for a paycheck job, and for some, a client may be the transition they need to go back to the employment world.

A bit of a hybrid between the independent consulting and full-time job world is to serve as a consultant in a bigger firm. These are local, regional or national companies with a cadre of women and men who go from client to client at the direction of the company. In this case you might get a regular paycheck (W-2) or paid like a contractor (1099). If you're a contractor with a bigger firm, then you might be part time - working a set number of hours per day, days per week or until the job is done, then you wait for them to call you again.

If you're not full-time, then you're part-time, and part-time consultants come in a number of stripes. The circumstances which surround part-time consulting are wide and varied. What they all have in common is picking up supplemental income and maintaining, building or sharpening your skill set.

You might be working "on the side" while maintaining your full-time job. Some have asked me whether this is ethical, since in areas like fundraising, you could help your client compete for the same money as your employer. This is where full disclosure, and some good sense comes in. Let everyone know what's going on so you don't put yourself at risk.

You could also have other obligations that you need to work around, like children's schedules or elder care, so you have a limited number of hours to devote to your consulting activities? You could be at the end of your career or retired from a regular job. Part-time consulting is a good way to stay meaningfully active without the obligations of a full-time employment – plus get supplemental income for household expenses or travel.

Why is all of this important? Because your reason for consulting can impact what you charge, your time availability, and even your reliability to get work done for your client. (If you have a full-time job and are consulting on the side, for example can you take a call at work from a consulting client with an emergency?) If the money you earn is a supplement to a greater income from retirement, a spouse, or other revenue, may not feel pressured to charge as much as those who rely on consulting as a full-time primary household income. On the other hand, if you have a consulting practice as a full-time business, your ability to serve customers may be greater because you have no other outside responsibilities to fulfill.

As a consultant to a nonprofit, how you approach your consulting, whether part-time or full-time, may not make a difference to your client. However, understanding your commitment to consulting can make a major difference to how you approach your work.

Exercise 7

Define the kind of consultant you want to be in the short and long term.

I define Short Term as (number of weeks/months/years): _____

I define Long Term as (by what date or year?): _____

Exercise 8

After reviewing the section above…

In the Short Term I will be this kind of consultant: (PT/FT, another descriptor?)

_____

In the Long Term I will be this kind of consultant: (PT/FT, another descriptor?)

_____

2 INFRASTRUCTURE (BACK OFFICE)

Your Vision and Mission

We've already talked about what you want out of a consulting practice focused on nonprofits. You've looked at whether you see this as full-time or part-time work. Now let's sum it up in a way that could be familiar to you if you come from the nonprofit sector, and what might be new to you if you don't.

What's your vision and mission?

Remember, a "vision" is a statement of an ideal world where the issue you are concerned about is solved. Your mission is how you set out to make your vision a reality.

What's an ideal world look like for your consulting to nonprofits? Like we said above, are you consulting because...

- You want to test out a new career direction?

- Your tired of working for other people?

- You can't find the kind of job you want, or are tired of constantly being number two in the interview process?

- You want to prove something to yourself or your professional colleagues?

- You simply want a means to earn extra cash?

None of these are bad reasons to enter consulting. It's just important to know which ones (or any beyond these) are considerations in your decision. Whatever your reasons are, it will have a major influence on how you develop your consulting practice, and how you interact with clients. They all influence your "vision" for your work.

How about your mission? What do you expect to do to make your vision come true? Will you help organizations build a planned giving program? Will you serve a number of nonprofits as their interim chief financial officer? Maybe you will get social service nonprofits in line with the latest state treatment guidelines? Whatever it is, be specific, and brief, in how you intend to work with nonprofits to help them address their mission.

Exercise 9

For your work as a nonprofit consultant, in no more than three sentences (one sentence would be great!), write your...

Vision statement:

_____

_____

_____

_____

_____

Exercise 10

Mission statement:

_____

_____

_____

_____

_____

Like any nonprofit, now that you have your mission and vision in place, it's time to plan.

Building your plan

Business planning is a long, laborious, soul-sucking task that rates right up there with doing taxes, right? Only if you make it that way. Really, you can come out smiling. Let's review what the popular planning methods:

- **Wing it! Make no plan.**

Right up there with the tru-ism that most people do not have wills, I'd venture a guess that most businesses do not have plans… of any sort. This is a mistake. As they say, "failing to plan is planning to fail." And no, having it "all right here" while pointing to your head is not a plan!

- **A traditional business plan.**

Many traditional business startup guides suggest that having a business plan is one of the first, and best things you can do to begin your enterprise. I don't necessarily argue with this, but I think it is important for you to keep some things in mind as you consider doing a business plan, and if you decide to move forward with it.

Business plan advocates say that a business plan will:

- Force you to step back and look at your business concept more realistically.

- Push you to systematically review your competitors and their strengths and weaknesses.

- Help you build an infrastructure to support your enterprise.

- Make you be more realistic about your revenue stream.

These are all good reasons for a business plan.

Those against business plans will tell you that:

- Business plans really aren't for you, they're for your investors. If you are in a business that will sooner than later require a substantial influx of cash, having a business plan is essential. No investor, whether that's a bank, a venture capitalist or your brother-in-law, will consider giving you money to build your business unless you have a well thought out plan.

- You will find that creating a business plan will take a substantial amount of time, which is keeping you out of the business you want to pursue.

- Business plans tend to stifle creativity. Rather than helping you "think outside the box," business plans keep you in the box and away from opportunities.

- Business plans are all about modeling ideal events, like amounts of revenue. The problem is unless you are experienced in the business you are going into; you will not have an idea of how much revenue you will bring in.

Personally, having gone through the exercise of building a business plan, I found it a bit frustrating that my business paradigm changed so quickly so early in my business' age. While a formal business plan was an interesting exercise, it was fundamentally useless within six months of its completion. Therefore, I'm not suggesting that you don't need to have a plan for your business. I'm just asking you to consider whether a formal business plan is right for you.

- **A Lean Startup**

It might be worth considering the "lean startup" paradigm as put forward by Eric Reis in 2011 in his book "The Lean Startup." After starting several failed businesses using the traditional, well considered business plan approach, Reis realized that despite his careful planning, something was wrong. He found, counter-intuitively, that he invested too much time planning for the results he was getting. That led him to Lean Startup.

Reis is careful to say that the Lean Startup concept is not "wing it," non-planning. It involves careful thought, and with that, more action than paper. Reis wants you to learn your market, test your market, follow your market and be willing to give up your plans for your market's need.

This can be a problem, because you like your idea for your business. Consider, however, that people see you differently than you see yourself. They might see what you're good at before you do... and you'll be happier doing what you're good at.

Exercise 11

Using outside sources, decide on the type of plan that's good for your business as a consultant to nonprofits. Provide the rationale here:

_____

_____

_____

_____

_____

And while you're at it, how about goals?

Setting business goals five ways

We all should know what a goal is, right? In the broadest sense, a goal is a different "state of being" from your present condition. Goals imply "improvement" and "progress." Wherever you are... say, "Point A," then your goal is to be at "Point B," and we imagine "Point B" to be a better state by however you measure it. Point B is your goal.

For many of us, we learned about goals in our "paycheck job." It could be someone taught us that goals should be "SMART:" Specific, Measurable, Achievable, Realistic and Timely. Whether in nonprofits or business, it was likely that each year you set goals, and each year you reviewed goals. (And each year, maybe your salary or other kind of incentive was tied to your meeting one or more goals.)

Now that you're on your own, while you probably acknowledge that goals are good, you may not find setting goals that urgent compared to everything else to do. After all, you're "independent," right? You've cast off the shackles of a large, overbearing employer. It's just you, and you know what it means to do better for you, right?

Well, kind of.

If that's working for you, super. Stop reading here, if for no other reason than you'll probably not pay attention to the rest anyhow.

For everyone else... read on. Let's talk about the kind of goals you want to set.

- **Monetary Goals**:

For a lot of us, this is the first thing that comes to mind. Are you meeting your goals for money? Most small business owners have one measure: did I pay my bills?

After that, goals for money are easy to ignore. You might even think they're beyond your control. While there's a kernel of truth to that, you probably serve nonprofits that have some cycle to their work. Are there specific times of the year when you can either work with a client vs. avoiding them entirely because they're serving their own clients? For example, we know that food banks feed people all year 'round. But I'd be especially careful approaching them around the holidays. They're inundated with food intake from food drives, food distribution or managing volunteers who only show up once a year. If they're a major client type, your goals need to reflect a downtime in business in December, but maybe an up-tick in October when you're helping them prepare for the deluge.

- **Client Contact Goals:**

How often do you reach out to clients, even if just to say "hi?" How many networking events do you go to? Are you a member of organizations that relate to your client base? Client contacts come in all shapes and sizes, personal contact at big networking events or one to one over coffee, to a quick call to their office or an email or note card. The point is to be intentional about making contact, however you define a "contact." Don't leave contacting clients, a function that keeps you and your brand "top of mind," to chance... unless you want your work to come in by chance, too.

- **Lifestyle Goals:**

Does your business support the lifestyle you want for yourself? Are you living in a manner that brings you personal and professional comfort now, and lets you save for doing the same in the future when maybe you don't want to, or can't do what you're doing now? Some of you might say, "isn't lifestyle driven by money?" Yes, and... While every lifestyle requires a certain income to support it, you also need intent. Even if you're doing quite well, if your spouse is a teacher who gets summers off and your business doesn't support your dream of taking summers off, too, you're not meeting your lifestyle goals.

- **Programmatic Goals:**

What kind of work are you doing and is it the kind of work you like to do? For example, maybe you're a management consultant who helps nonprofit staff maximize their potential. Is that the kind of work that suits you? Are you doing the kind of work that maximizes your own talents and interests? Do you feel energized most of the time when you do your work? What are your goals for doing more of the work that you're great at, and less of the work you aren't?

- **Missional Goals:**

Rarely does this come up in business, but when you're working with nonprofits, you might ask: Does my work contribute to missions that inspire my passion? Are you getting clients that make you want to get up in the morning and serve their needs? It's one of the benefits of being in a business that serves people who do great things. There's no reason you can't have some of that rub off on you.

Whether you use these categories as a place to start or find others that suit you better, setting goals could be one of the most important steps in building a business that reflects your personality, and serves your needs.

Exercise 12

Name three goals in each of the categories list. Add categories if necessary:

Monetary Goals:

_____

_____

_____

Client Contact Goals:

_____

_____

_____

Lifestyle Goals:

_____

_____

_____

Programmatic Goals:

_____

_____

_____

Missional Goals:

_____

_____

_____

Other Category 1: _____

_____

_____

_____

Other Category 2: _____

_____

_____

_____

Gathering your team.

Successful nonprofit consulting does not exist in a vacuum, and meeting those goals doesn't happen alone. Support for your physical, mental/emotional, financial, legal and business needs means putting a team of people in place who can bring their expertise to bear in ways that will allow you to focus on your core business.

You'll need other advisers, some of which you will be in regular contact, others who you'll talk to maybe once a year, so your work occurs smoothly and your clients are happy. (While touched on below, accounting and legal members of your team are addressed in more detail elsewhere in the book.)

Here are what I feel are at least the basics:

Physical Health professionals: Get a clean bill of physical health. Make certain that whatever issues you're facing physically are managed, and that you can do physically what's needed to improve your emotional resilience. We're talking about regular exercise, regardless of the season or your work load. I know too well that it's easy to say "tomorrow" when a deadline looms.

Just getting a basic checkup may be a challenge for a nonprofit consultant. Your health care may have gone away with your paycheck job. Don't let that stop you. Take full advantage of public resources so you can get at least fundamental healthcare.

Mental Health professionals: There's a lot of stigma and fear around mental health that prevents folks from seeking assistance before issues get bigger than they otherwise should. Fear, anxiety, depression… they can all come with the consulting/freelancing turf. If there's anything a successful consultant could use on his or her toughest days, is an objective third party to offer proven, creative tools to address what can seem like a "bigger than life" issue.

Consider also that some mental health professionals (and coaches - see below) use evaluation tools in their work, like the Myers-Briggs or another. Understanding your preferences in how you work and interact with others could be valuable as you meet the wide variety of people that you're likely to encounter in nonprofit consulting.

I'm not suggesting that you run right out and line up a counselor. However, as someone who works with nonprofits, you may be in a position to hear of resources that you can take advantage of when you need it. Circling back to above, the first place to start maybe your physical health professional: your physician. S/he can recommend someone that other patients use.

As for the cost? Mental health is increasingly covered by insurance plans, although often not with parity. There are also sliding scale (often nonprofit) services available. While it may not be an official "business expense" (ask your accountant or tax professional), it makes good business sense to seek help if you feel it would be useful.

Friends: Friends are great, and everybody needs 'em. They'll come from a variety of sources… people you know from your neighborhood, your kids school, or always knew since childhood. You could have relationships from your last paycheck job that have endured since you left. Over time, you may have developed professional acquaintances in the same or complementary disciples, whom you see, socially. Since they're friends, and assuming you want to keep it that way, just be cautious about the amount of whining and complaining, or even enthusiasm, about your lifestyle. All of these can be a source of support, and a valuable network leading to clients. However, never put a personal friend in a position to connect you with business unless you are 100% certain that they want to. If they aren't comfortable about helping, they may do it once, and you'll never see them again.

Except for friends who are also consultants in the same way you are, even your friends will misunderstand your choice to consult, what consulting means to your finances, and how consulting is expressed in your available time, just to name a few. You'll find yourself clearing up a lot of misunderstandings, and you'd be surprised when an "educational moment" presents itself. Even after years of consulting, I've discover that many friends don't really grasp what I do, or that I may not be available when they are. Don't be surprised that some will "just let you know" about the paycheck jobs they see. Take it as an act of misguided love. They want you to have a happy, stable life, just like them.

Spouse/Partner, Boy/Girlfriends: To those with whom you have a closer, more intimate relationship, your consulting work can be fraught with misunderstandings and frustration, and joy and fascination. "We can't go out because you have a client's board meeting tonight?" "Who was that wo/man on the phone and what did she want?" "We have to wait to buy that deck furniture until after your quarterlies are paid?" "Oh, I can come to the five-star event as your guest?"

Treat these people in your life like the saints you hope they will be. They are your first line of defense against the issues that come up daily. They are also the first people to celebrate your success. Know also, like your friends, your partner will not fully grasp your life - good and bad - unless you share it. Consider also that complaining too much or effusing too much (and only you and him/her can determine "too much") to your spouse or partner can be a fast track to ending your relationship - another good reason to consider a professional counselor. Venting to a third party could be the buffer your spouse/partner relationship needs.

Professional Service Advisers: Like noted elsewhere in this book, bankers, accountants, and attorneys live their lives very much like you might – on networking and referrals. Each could recommend one of the others (like your banker can recommend an accountant) who specializes in working with consultants and freelancers at a price you can afford. However, price is not everything. You want someone who knows how to work with "micro-businesses" of one, two or three people. If they work with nonprofits, they could be a source of referrals, too.

Life and business coaches: This is in increasingly popular source of support for many people. Because the field is new, and largely unlicensed, and usually not heavily credentialed, you need to qualify those who offer these services. While they may seem like "therapists lite," they should not offer services that could be interpreted as psychological counseling. In fact, a good coach should be able to refer you to someone if s/he sees signs of your needing help beyond their skill set. Go into the relationship with a specific set of objectives, especially if you are seeking business advice. For example, if you need marketing help, is that their specialty? Also, have a prearranged concept that you both agree upon for knowing when you are "done." That might mean when your first 1000 people sign up for your newsletter, for example. This doesn't mean you can't extend your relationship, but that you have a benchmark to revisit it.

Mentors: You could think of a mentor as a "volunteer coach." Yet whether a formal ("will you be my mentor") or informal (someone with more experience who is your "go to guy" for feedback) it is important to make it a two-way relationship. You may not be able to offer as much at first. Over time you should be able to discern what is valuable to your mentor so that s/he doesn't see you as someone who takes all of the time. This maybe something as simple as a heartfelt thank you, a business referral, or recognition when you stand up to receive an award as the "Top Nonprofit Consultant of the Year." (Hmmm... let's start that!)

Identifying a mentor can be tricky. Unlike some professional organizations with mentor/mentee programs for people in their specific disciplines (like many chapters of the Association of Fundraising Professionals do), few (if any) exist for nonprofit consulting. Maybe more important, your colleague consultants may not be open to the idea as much as you hoped.

First of all, as you know, "time is money." Time spent with you would not be billable, so it is a potential loss of income.

Second, from their point-of-view, a mentor relationship for consulting might seem for the prospective mentor like giving away all of his/her secrets to the new competition in the field.

This is the same issue that faced anyone entering the crafts before the industrial revolution. Formal, guild-endorsed, apprenticeships addressed that problem. A blacksmith would give up the secrets of his trade only to someone he was formally engaged with as a student, of sorts. Assuming that you do not want to live at your mentor's home for seven years as an apprentice, what can you do?

Consider a formal business relationship. Some consultants, late in their careers, will partner with a junior person who may (or may not) buy their business later. In the meantime, you can subcontract on "lesser" jobs as an adjunct to his/her work with clients, all the while picking up the experience you need. This is a rare arrangement, but potentially fruitful for both parties if you find an interested senior consultant.

Business Associations: Another source of support is your local business association. This could be a community service club, like Rotary or Lions, or a formal networking group, like BNI (Business Network International) or a chamber of commerce. Look also for organizations that may encourage business opportunities among those with your shared gender, ethnicity or religion. You could also form your own group with like-minded nonprofit consultants, freelancers or other solo/small business people in your area. Whether local or national, specialized or general, look for one that shares your business values and could provide access to your idea market. While getting to know plumbers and shopkeepers could be handy, you may be better off connected to other businesses who also do business with nonprofits, like bankers, architects and event planners.

Business support organizations: Your local SCORE, SBA Centers and nonprofit business creation organization live for business. They're a great place for support in getting started, and for issues that can come up along the way. SCORE (www.score.org, whose name came from "Service Corps of Retired Executives") brands itself as "Counselors to America's Small Business." Chances are that there is a chapter office near you.

The SBA, the US Government's Small Business Administration, also has offices around the country, and a very close relationship with SCORE. Go to www.sba.gov for a variety of resources.

Besides these national organizations, many communities have independent nonprofits who support business creation and sustainability through counseling, classes, networking and online resources. Your local chamber of commerce or banker may be a place to start. Also, don't get put off by an organization's name that may not include your personal demographic. Key to starting my business was a nonprofit whose name started with the word "women." It turns out that they welcomed anyone into their classes, regardless of gender, and that my tuition was subsidized by a state grant they won.

Technology Adviser: Today, at some level – from basic to highly sophisticated – you're likely to need help with your technologies. At your paycheck job, that meant calling the IT department and dropping everything if someone showed up. As a consultant, this won't be an option. When something goes wrong, you'll need to consider the trade-offs between what you can do yourself, what you can do yourself but don't want or have the time to do, and what you can't imagine doing at all. This will include your computer hardware and software. That's why it is important to at least identify a computer hardware/software technician who is versed in your system type (Apple, Windows, Android, etc.) Make sure that you understand the pricing structure, feel confident about any data integrity and/or privacy issues, and timing of any work done. Of the three, timing is, in my opinion, extremely important (and a good reason to use cloud computing.) Will losing your machine to the shop for several days grind your consulting to a halt? If you need, can the shop give you a loaner? Do you have a back-up machine for your own use?

Use these checklists as a way to gather your team and get yourself ready for consulting:

Exercise 13

Physician:

___ If necessary, arrange for health insurance and identify a physician.
___ Get a checkup.
___ Tell your physician that you are considering (or doing) consulting.
___ Follow all medical advice and lifestyle recommendations.

Exercise 14

Mental Health Professional:

___ Inquire with your health insurance company about your coverage for, and process to engage mental health services.

Exercise 15

Spouse/Partner, Boy/Girlfriends:

___ Hold an "education summit" (in a single block of time, or a series of scheduled smaller time periods) about your interest in, or work in, nonprofit consulting. Have a written agenda. Discuss time commitments, financial implications and how your work will impact your relationship and the relationship and availability to your family. Make sure you cover the benefits and the pitfalls - not just all the good new or bad news.

___ If you have children, discuss many of the same points at the level at which they will understand, and where it impacts their life. Be sure to listen to their concerns. You could be surprised at what they bring up. (It may go from the global "will we starve" to the immediate "okay, but can you pick me at Jimmy's tomorrow.")

____ If you imagine significant changes in lifestyle or finances, or if your child reacts in an unusual way, consider making your children's teacher or school counselor aware of your consulting business and how it has impacted your family situation.

Exercise 16

Friends:

____ Develop a script to describe your consulting plans work to friends and extended family. Be ready for expressions and questions like "are you crazy," "great, now you can pick up my kids after school," and "I could never do that." Ask them why they said or asked what they did and explain how your change may impact them. Also, emphasize that while your work could be more flexible and the place could be at home, it is still work that needs to be accomplished, just like theirs.

Exercise 17

Professional Service Advisers:

____ Make a list of three accountants, three lawyers from your discussions with your banker, friends and colleagues. Make an appointment to interview at least two of each.

____ Visit with the manager of your current bank's branch to discuss your plans for consulting and the support services they offer. Visit one other bank to compare services.

Exercise 18

Life and business coaches:

____ Create a list of all aspects of your business which may benefit from coaching.

Exercise 19

Mentors:

____ Identify and make a list of the people who are established in consulting or freelancing in your specialty through internet searches, LinkedIn or business associations.

____ Learn about the reputation and work of these people through your current business friends and colleagues.

____ At upcoming networking events, connect with one or more of these potential mentors.

____ Select two to meet with over coffee, lunch or another time.

Exercise 20

Business Associations:

____ Identify and make a list of local or national business associations and specialty professional associations through an internet search and inquiry with your business colleagues. (Members of ThinkNP.com get a list of professional organizations with their membership.)

____ Inquire about their "guest" policy to attend an upcoming meeting and the costs and commitment for full membership.

____ Attend one meeting of a business or professional association that you have never attended before.

Exercise 21

Business support organizations:

____ Make a list of all SBA, SCORE and/or local business encouragement organizations within driving distance.

Exercise 22

Technology Adviser:

____ Create a list of computer repair companies in your area. Ask the following:

Do they work on your type of machine? Y/N: ____

What is the average time before a repair can be started (not completed, just started)? # Days: ____

Do they offer loaner machines while yours is being repaired? Y/N: ____

What is their pricing structure? Price per hour: _____. Per job price list? Y/N: ____

Did you get a copy (or see on website) of their data integrity and information privacy? Y/N: ____

Do they pick up, or must you take your machine to them? Y/N: ___

For software issues, can they diagnose and work with your machine, remotely? Y/N: ___

Your business works for you!

There are a lot of days when it is easy to forget that your business works for you. What I mean by that? Think of the days when you have to do the things that you're not real thrilled about doing. Maybe that's accounting? It could be writing advertising copy. Is it replying to RFP? Whatever it is, you get stressed out about the process or the results. It's easy to say to yourself "I have to do this for the business" and slog through, producing a less-than-stellar product. While that may be true, remember that you're in charge. The business works for you. Put in place the processes that work for you, or get people to do the work that you disdain or have no talent for. That way you can do what you're good at, have more fun, and get better results (and be able to pay for that help.)

Unlike working in the business sector, working for the nonprofit sector has an alternative: volunteering. If you are serious about consulting, you don't want to volunteer unless you really want to. Confusion on this point is easy.

More than one starting consultant has told me how their potential client assumed they were volunteering their time, not charging for it. Whose mistake is that? The consultants! Yes, there may be some "willful ignorance" on the part of the nonprofit. Still, it's the responsibility of the consultant to clear that up right from the start. Saying something like "I'm happy to meet with you for an hour or so to assess your situation to see where I can help." [followed by] "After that we can talk about a contract between us."

You know that in the end, consulting is a business. As such, it needs to produce income for your personal goals. If you are not producing revenue and a profit at some point, your accountant, or worse yet, an IRS auditor will say that you are no longer in business and strip you of the rights and privileges of the organization. This means that you need to take it seriously and treat it like a business.

Being in your own business is what separates you from your last job, and your current (or soon-to-be) nonprofit clients. In the past, somebody else worried about the organization's cash flow, accounting, or marketing while you could focus on your specialty and the weekly paycheck that came with it. Today, all those concerns are yours and the paycheck may not come nearly as often.

If it looks and acts like a business, then treat it like one.

What's your image of a business? This is very important. If you grew up in a family that always depended on jobs from employers for its income, your view of "business" is very different from someone who watched a family member in their own enterprise. It could be that your only contact with a business owner is your boss, several layers above you, or the local laundry or restaurant. If you've spent a while working for a nonprofit, any business owners you know are successful donors, or maybe your board members. They may be good role models. Just remember that rarely did you see them at tough times in their business. Board meetings and donor visits are hardly the times a business owner gripes about a lost contract or brings up a tough personnel issue.

Why does this matter? Your experience with business and business owners will shape how you see your own business - what to expect from it, what you can't expect from it, and how you treat your role in it.

Exercise 23

Name five impressions you have of "business" and the people who own them.

_____

_____

_____

_____

_____

Exercise 24

Define "success" for your business.

_____

_____

_____

_____

Exercise 25

What three traits would you like your business to have?

_____

_____

_____

What you may have observed, and what was said above (remember 60-30-10?) is that there are three primary functions that any consultant needs to balance in their business:

- Doing the work - what you think of as "consulting."

- Telling others what you do so that you get clients - known as marketing and sales.

- Doing the accounting, list keeping, contracts and etc. - what some people call "back office" or infrastructure.

As an independent consultant, when you do one, you are not doing the other two. It's important to know that this juggling act will keep you occupied for a substantial part of your consulting life.

Michael Gerber, in his best-selling book "The E-Myth Revisited" makes a point (among several excellent ones) that it is as essential to work "on" your business as it is "in" your business. What is "on" and "in"?

"In" is what (I hope) you love to do. It's why you started your consulting to begin with. Maybe you're an accountant or a fundraisers or a designer. It's doing that.

"On" is everything else you need to do so you can do the "in." That's the billing, the marketing, maintaining the technology and much, much more. You might say it's the business of the business.

What most of us don't see unless we've seen a business owner up close, is how much "on" happens and contributes to the success of the business. In fact, the "in" part might make up only a small proportion of the owner's time. Sometimes what we define as "success" is the ability to leave the "in" to someone else. At what point did Bill Gates stop writing code and focus exclusively on the "on"? Maybe he always hated code and had more fun with marketing, sales and finance?

As a consultant, freelancer or vendor to nonprofits, especially if you're independent, and especially if you're starting out, you'll do a lot of "in." That's good, because that's why you got into the work to begin with. If you're lucky, like if you get an ongoing stream of referrals, you'll be able to stay that way - doing nearly all "in" and little "on." Again, this depends on how you see business, and especially your business.

If "success" is doing fundraising campaigns for the rest of your life, and one after another, they come to you - then great! You'll do less "on" and more "in."

If "success" is building a cadre of consultants who you enlist to manage campaigns while you look for the next - then great! You'll do less "in" and more "on."

It's all up to you... and you can change the ratio at any time. Just know that you may be able to eliminate the "in" from your life, but rarely the "on." If it's fun, all the better.

However, you create the in/on ratio, remember that because you can do something doesn't mean you should. Some of what you do is better assigned to someone else.

Exercise 26

Complete this four-square grid:

	Like it	Hate it
Good at it		
Not Good at it		

- If you are not good at something and hate doing it, unless you're pushed to do the activity, don't do it. Outsource that job to someone else who loves it, or at minimum, automate all or part of the work, if that's possible.

- If you're not good at something but love it, consider your time an opportunity to learn so you get good at it. This is an area where you should seek a mentor, or take a class.

- If you're good at something but hate it, minimize your time doing that task, only do it for the best of reasons, and if it is some aspect of your client work, charge more than average when you must do it. Maybe you should supervise others doing this function?

- Being good at something and loving it is your sweet spot. Build your business on it.

You might be doing activities in the first three bullets above because you think you have to. Maybe someone told you "that's what business is," or you're thinking "I can't afford to have someone else do it." Maybe.

My (informed) guess is that you will find your effectiveness increase, your business grows and your attitude toward it will improve, if you take off your plate what you are not good at, or don't like doing. If you can make money doing what you love and are good at, the cost of outsourcing what's in the other three quadrants goes down, especially in relation to what you can make.

And what underpins all of this? Where you work…

Your own space

Let's face it: nonprofit employees don't toil in ideal working conditions. I've seen too many cramped offices with 20-year-old glossy pale green cinder block walls housing too many oversized steel desks with too many wires running above, feeding last year's technology.

That's why, if you come into B2N consulting from a nonprofit, you may be one of the few types of consultants where your work conditions actually improve by going on your own! While the most obvious improvement is the physical space of your office, you also need to protect your temporal space (otherwise known as "time"), too.

Let's start with physical space...

You start with a basic decision: home, or not home.

Home Offices

Even something as simple as "home" brings a handful of choices.

There's the improvised office: The kitchen counter, dining room table and comfy living room chair. Each of these may be a nice supplement to another environment, too.

Then there's the "formal" home office: the spare bedroom, partitioned dining room or basement, enclosed porch or garage.

Advantages of working at home are:

- Low/no cost. This is huge when starting out. Being able to keep costs to a minimum puts more money in your pocket.

- Possible tax advantages. See your accountant on advice on this. You may be able to apportion part of your home - whether you rent or own - as business space.

- No commute. According to USA Today, the average American commute time is 25.5 minutes. That's nearly an hour a day. Just think what you could do with that spare hour… or five hours a week, or more than a full day a month!

(http://www.usatoday.com/story/news/nation/2013/03/05/americans-commutes-not-getting-longer/1963409/)

- Focus on projects requiring undivided attention. When you're at home, nobody's passing by your cube, asking whether you saw the game last night.

- Availability to family responsibilities. Need to run the kids to school, or mom to the doctor? You can work around it.

Disadvantages:

- It's lonely: For some people, working at home is like being in solitary confinement. If you thrive on interactions with others, being at home all day could be a major issue.

- Location: Maybe you don't live in a place that's conducive to a home-office. You could be far away from your clients, or you have neighbors that don't respect your privacy?

- Space: Is there simply no space where you live that you can carve out for an office?

- Regulations: Are there municipal zoning regulations or business license requirements in your area that discourage home-offices?

- Family: Do you have family issues that make working at home impossible? If your family is around when work's to be done, then there's pressure to interact. Putting up boundaries - emotional if not physical or at least temporal - is key to creating a place where you can produce your best work.

- Procrastination: Oh, but being at home brings all sorts of temptations to procrastinate. First, there's "outside media." I'll define that as television, radio, maybe Netflix and even eBay, Amazon and social media. Then there's life's "background noise." Need to run a load of wash? Dishes in the sink? Want to cook a snack? Straighten up the living room, kid's room, your room? If you love to procrastinate, all of these are deadly. Being able to regulate yourself, or better yet, ignore them until when the rest of the world does these tasks, is key to accomplishing your day's work.

- You: Do you need separation from work and home so that you have a balanced life? Is your work style one where "going to work" helps you get things done? Maybe your home is your "safe haven?" Many of us use home - and rightly so - as a get-away place where we can leave the stresses of work. This is healthy. By making your home your work environment, you lose that safe haven to the demands of clients and the ever present computer or desk.

- Societal norms. When I look out the window and see everyone else commuting, I confess some mixed feelings. On one hand, I have a slight pang of exclusion as I see everyone else heading someplace seemingly important, each day. That's quickly overcome by realizing the time and money I save. Plus, I'm much more environmentally friendly, right?

- Clients: Do your clients expect you to have a "professional" space where they can meet you?

Exercise 27

Evaluate your home for work space possibilities. What's open or what can you adjust so you can have a space to write, read and reflect?

_____

_____

_____

_____

_____

While it's true that today's virtual business environment can take us anywhere (and don't we all imagine ourselves communicating with clients from a tropical paradise?) the reality is that working from anywhere – especially at home – may not be as practical as it seems. Rather than washing up an idyllic shore, you more likely beached at the dining room table.

What's the alternative?

Outside-the-home space

Once you step outside your house, the possibilities increase, and so do the cost. It's important that you know exactly why you want to bear the expense.

Here are some of your options:

Small towns offer interesting possibilities. You might find something above a store or restaurant, or in a district or town where there's mixed zoning between residential and business. A lot of these are independently rented by the owner who might run the other business in the same building, or a small business person who holds several local properties.

These are in contrast to **office parks or free-standing office buildings** with available space. Often these are rented by the companies who own multiple buildings of a similar type, or serve as rental agents representing properties throughout your region. The price goes up in these situations, but so does the "look and feel" of the environment. Sometimes you'll see this kind of space listed as "Class A" office space.

A client could offer space. Once a good relationship is established with a client, (or a client's volunteer, I have found) they may be glad to have you work in their space once-in-a-while, after your job with them is done. This is a nice privilege that is good to keep in the back of your mind if you really need a place in a pinch.

In the same way, you could be a bit more formal. I know a few consultants who have a **permanent "sub-office" in someone else's location**. In other words, they rent from someone who has an office suite who has an available office space. Think of this like having a room in a boarding house. It's a less expensive alternative, but since you'll be interacting with your "neighbors" on a regular basis, you need to consider their habits in your decision. This arrangement might also come with some minor support functions, like access to coffee, a kitchenette, copying and the like. You might approach a local nonprofit who is interested in some extra income

(Caution: renting out space might trigger unrelated business income tax (UBIT) for the nonprofit. If they already pay UBIT for another activity, then they may not have extra accounting costs with your occupation of their space. If they don't, or don't understand the process, the nonprofit may turn you down on that basis. Encourage them to ask their accountant before making a decision.)

Akin to this but dressed up a bit more is **leased space from an office suite company**. This differs from a "sub-office" in that the entire operation is geared to people like you, who might need an office, just not their own, exclusive office suite. There's usually a scale of services. You can get a full, exclusive and dedicated office that nobody else will ever occupy. You can get access to an office that you would occupy when needed (kind of a "hotel" arrangement.) Maybe you just get an office cube? These can also come with a full complement of amenities, like copying, a desk attendant to answer your phone, a reserve-able conference room, mail services, a kitchenette and more. All of this means that you get a menu of pricing based on the options you select.

In some bigger cities, you can find a **co-working spaces**. It's somewhat similar to what I've already described, with many of the same amenities. The difference I observe is that they try to encourage a collaborative atmosphere, and may focus their energies on a specific market, like "creative professionals," women, or those who work with nonprofits.

Moving down the expense scale there are at least two other options.

The first are **membership organizations** to consider. City clubs, chambers of commerce and other organizations to which you may already belong (or now will consider joining) can have space they offer to members as "quick offices." These are where you can make calls privately or spend some time at a desk or comfortable chair using their Wi-Fi connection. These are decidedly temporary arrangements, but you might be a "regular" and nobody will mind.

The local café (examples are national chains like Starbucks or Panera Bread) or other places you can "hang out" with a Wi-Fi connection. Many places welcome "campers" (as I heard a barista call everyone with a laptop) and others do not. (In busier locations of some they restrict Wi-Fi time.) I think of these as "alone with others" spaces. They can be an interesting landing place for a getaway when home is not an option. However, they can be noisy and not at all private when you have a call to take or make, and you risk being spotted by friends and neighbor who take an opportunity to talk (and talk and talk.) Especially in privately owned shops, try not to take valuable, peak-time seat space if you're not buying something appropriate to the time-of-day. If you and others regularly buy nothing through the lunch hour, they won't be in business for you for too long.

Libraries are hugely underutilized resources. Budget cutback have made many unattractive, but today nearly all come with free Wi-Fi in addition to free computers to use. Plus, the right library could have resources to help your project, like the Foundation Center online directory.

Each of these outside-the-home spaces has advantages and disadvantages specific to their configuration and how you use them. In general, consider:

Advantages:

- Collegial atmosphere. You might need others around you, even for part of the day. That's okay.

- Amenities. Conference rooms, coffee, receptionist, mail box and more. For some people, where they work needs to feel like "work."

- Networking. Some of the above named spaces encourage interaction for mutual benefit, If you're starting out, this could be a serious advantage. If you're established, it could be a great ongoing conduit for clients.

Disadvantages:

- Too collegial/interruptions. There's a fine line. On one hand, you want to know people and feel welcome. On the other, you have deadlines to meet and prospects meetings to prepare for.

- Expense. Most of these options cost money… even the cost of some coffee or a bagel.

- Noise. Noise is interesting. White noise can be comforting and help you work. If you don't like your project, or are running out of energy, you might find yourself listening to someone else's conversation instead of doing your own work.

I'm sure you can come up with more.

You have to work somewhere. Selecting the right place can mean the difference between a productive day (and business) and spinning your wheels. Consider also that a wise choice may be some combination of the above.

Exercise 28

Review the above list. Name three possibilities that offer good alternatives for you to a home office.

_____

_____

_____

Your Time

Just as important as physical space is your time. Consulting is going to take a major adjustment for you, your loved ones and your friends.

Starting today you own your time… and with ownership comes responsibility.

The physical removal from one's self from home to go to work is a very industrial age concept - at most 250 years old, and for most families, less than 100 - a minor blip in human history. Today, most paycheck jobs expect you separate yourself physically from home, which for many, means you also separate yourself mentally. Like a good habit, one (the physical separation) triggers the other (the mental separation) resulting in a reward (your paycheck). Once consulting, unless you buy or rent yourself an office to visit daily, that trigger is gone. This has a significant implication for your consulting.

Without "work" to go to, work is then only defined by time, not a space. That time need not all be in one block. In fact, if you examined your paycheck life closely, the time at work probably was not all one block, either. It's just that the "bumper times" between meetings, checking Facebook or catching up on your weekends with your co-workers, were all folded into your paycheck. As a consultant, you own those times, not your employer. And with that ownership, comes responsibility. It's still okay to take a 15-minute break for Twitter, now it's just 15 minutes you don't get paid for.

Until you focus yourself on the tasks at hand, preferably for a client but even for your broader consulting practice at hand (sales/marketing, billing, etc.), you're not working.

The problem with having work more connected with time and less with space is that it is easy to cheat. Laundry is a great example. Pop a load in... apply yourself to a client project... the buzzer rings. Move the laundry to the dryer... buzzer rings... take it and fold or hang because wrinkly clothes mean another step: ironing. One cycle, at least two interruptions in your focus, not to mention the errant thought "will it be done soon?" If you had a paycheck job, you wouldn't be around to do it. You'd do your laundry at night, maybe between another home task, like making dinner. Why not do the same, now?

Makes sense, right?

Maybe. The first person to convince that your work time is too valuable to spend doing the laundry, is you. What's your incentive? How about money? Consulting leads to a check... laundry leads to... more laundry? How about your client's mission? If you do the laundry and take more time completing your project, maybe your client can't feed as many children? If you get done your client work quickly, maybe you can spend more time with your family?

You can't blame others for this, either. Even if you just take the afternoon off from your paycheck work to get a job done for a client that you are working for "on the side," you're vulnerable to neighbors, friends and family deciding that you're available for their needs. Your first step is not to encounter them with this issue by growling "I'm working, don't bother me!" It is to convince yourself that your time is yours, not theirs, despite their perception of your being at home. Once you have yourself onboard, you can gently explain to others that you're at work, (saying "I'm on deadline" can make it sound more urgent) and that you'll circle back after "work hours," whenever you decide that is.

While we're talking about distractions that erode your time, let's talk about what maybe the most insidious: the electronics in our lives. This is really where you need to know yourself, and be honest with yourself at the same time.

Social media may come first to mind. Turn off alerts and notices. For many, television is a problem. For others, it's radio or recorded audio. It's a fine line. Having background media on can cut some of the feelings of isolation in the day.

Being honest with yourself means actually admitting that while you really like it, watching your favorite game show at 2 PM each afternoon really kills your productivity. It's quickly goes from being a treat that somehow you figure out how to give yourself daily, into a bad habit that erodes your ability to work with clients. Better to use that show as a motivation to make enough to invest in DVR (digital video recording) service.

Related, and just as essential, is knowing yourself. Brain science will tell us that the reason you find the background noise of talk radio distracting while you work (if you do), is that it uses the same brain pathways as the work you are trying to accomplish. Yet despite this information, it can take a lot of self-discipline to push the "off" button!

All of this sounds simple on paper, I know. The key, in my observation, is to know the value of your time and be persistent with yourself and others in protecting it. Sooner-than-later, you'll develop a good habit.

Of course, there are unavoidable issues that will take time away from your consulting. Just don't assume that because your client is an agency that helps parents with family issues that they will be empathic when it comes to yours. In my experience, nonprofits can be toughest on staff and consultants around issues that are related their mission.

For example, I know women employed by a women's and family advocacy organization who complained bitterly about the small level of support for their own family problems. I know youth organizations whose pressures on staff to produce results leads to a tremendous number of divorces. I won't speculate about why, and I am not suggesting this phenomenon is universal. Just know that "nonprofit" does not mean "soft." Meeting their deadline is imperative, despite what comes up in your life.

Exercise 29

Who in your life is most likely to demand time from you at times when you should normally put into your consulting practice?

_____

_____

_____

Name three steps to you need to take to have them see the importance of your consulting time.

_____

_____

_____

Office technology and equipment

Office equipment may be one of the few tangible expenses you will have as you build a consulting or freelance business serving nonprofits. If you're a vendor for other goods and services, you might have quite a bit more material to gather.

One of the nice things about this is that you may already own much of what you need. If you don't, for the basics like staplers and hole punchers, a chair or a desk, seriously consider going to a thrift store before you head to a big box office supply company or even an Internet source. I was surprised at what I could find over a couple of weeks at my local charity thrift store. I found an excellent desk which I've had for years, I regularly picked up binders that were in great shape, and found desktop file holders that serve me even now, 10 years later. People bring in all sorts of things, and if you regularly swing by, say once every other week or once a month, you should be able to populate your desktop at bargain prices. All the while, you are making a valuable contribution to the organization who sponsors the shop. And who knows? Maybe you'll find a nice shirt or pair of pants, to boot.

Exercise 30

_____ Visit a local thrift shop that has office material. Habitat for Humanity's Re-Stores often recycle desks and more, as do others. See what you can find for your office.

_____ While you're at it, connect with the organization's executive director to tell him/her that you're a consultant for nonprofits.

However, there are some things you can't find at a thrift shop, and you need to get the best you can afford. Technology is top on the list.

While it would be folly to recommend a specific computer for your work, it's certain that you will need one. If I were to mention an operating system, memory capacity or chip speed, they'd be obsolete before nearly as fast as I'm writing these words. However, I can say that you will need something that's fast enough, with sufficient capacity and storage space to handle the programs that you're likely to run and communicate with others. This is where having a good tech advisor comes in handy.

If your computer is your primary work tool, make a better-than-average investment in the product. If you're carrying it to meetings, then get something light. If you like to work in different spaces in your home, then get a larger laptop. If you're dealing in large photo files, invest in storage. Cheaping out on this purchase could cost you money, and time.

If you must spend less, consider a Chromebook (https://www.google.com/chromebook/). For the price, this Google internet device is very robust, and nearly disposable (or at least not too much that if it gets damaged, you won't be crushed.) Everything is backed up on Google's "Drive" cloud storage, and apps have evolved to integrate with the world's standard programs (like the Microsoft Suite.)

Related to office hardware is mobile hardware - tablets and phones. The cell phone is no longer considered a luxury good, particularly when it comes to business. Even a basic, clamshell cell phone is inadequate. You really need to have a smartphone so that you can interact with clients in a variety of ways while you are out of your office.

Some might put a tablet computer on the same list of essentials. It's certainly a major convenience, especially if you read e-books for the purposes of your business. That's up to you. What I find is that a tablet is a very convenient way to take notes, and much lighter in my briefcase or bag when I don't need a full keyboard.

Exercise 31

Review your technology. What pieces are missing or are in need of upgrade to effectively conduct your business?

_____

_____

_____

_____

_____

_____

Software

In his book "Go It Alone" Bruce Judson advocates for using software and other means to automate the back office functions of a small business to reduce costs and increase focus on the work at hand. This is even more possible today than it was in 2004 when Judson wrote his book.

Programs like Doodle serve well to coordinate schedules among people in different organizations. Eventbrite is an excellent way to manage events. Freshbooks or QuickBooks are the go-to programs for invoices. There are dozens of other programs that you may find useful, such as virtual fax machines, webinar/conference call programs, and many more. Some will be specific to your kind of work. Others will be specific to your nonprofit clients. Many of them are free, some of them will cost you a monthly fee. Be warned that the monthly fees can add up, so review your expenditures on a periodic basis.

Regardless of your type of work, or client type, there are some programs that are "must haves" when consulting. These include:

- Back up. Cloud storage is ubiquitous, at easily affordable monthly fees. Remember, you're not just working for you, you're working for your client. That means backing up information and keeping it secure, and even confidential. Skimping can cost you. Microsoft OneDrive, Google Drive, DropBox, Box, Amazon's Cloud and others all have reliable functionality.

- Anti-virus software. whether it's Norton, McAfee or another, there's no excuse. Your computer is your business life. Protect it.

- General word processing and etc. Microsoft Office suite. This is the de facto standard for spreadsheets, word processing, and more for more than a decade. While some like Google have made inroads, most of your clients are likely to use the Microsoft Suite in some iteration. As of this writing, it is available online, and in a downloadable version for a monthly fee. If you'd like to avoid that, consider Apache Openoffice. Openoffice is a similar suite of programs that is "open source" and free to the user. It has its own file extension, so anything you need to transfer to somebody else will need to be saved differently, usually in the Microsoft doc or xls format. You can find it at www.openoffice.org.

- Contact Managers. If you use Gmail or Microsoft Outlook, it is entirely possible to use the contacts function as a place to keep the names of your clients and some notes on them. At least this will work to start. Begin by listing everybody you know professionally in your contacts program. Think of the professional associations to which you belong, your colleagues at your current office, people you met at recent conferences and others.

Once your contact program becomes cumbersome, consider transferring them to a "CRM" (customer relationship management software.) Do a search to find when it's right for you. I know people who have had fine experience with Insightly.com, and others with Zoho.com. But there are dozens more out there, too. Get one that makes intuitive sense to you, at a price you can afford. Nearly all of these kinds of software are cloud based. Also, know that Insightly, Zoho and double as project management software, as well.

- Note keepers: A type of software that I have found essential, I call the "virtual file cabinet." Yet these do so much more than keeping documents. They also store photos, dictation, list, "clipped" internet articles and more. The major players in this type are Evernote and Microsoft OneNote.

Personally, I prefer Evernote. I know people who are just as passionate about OneNote. OneNote comes packaged with many Microsoft products. Evernote has a free version, although their Premium service is not too expensive.

Regardless of which you select, make sure you get a scanner to pair with the software. I have eliminated at least one four drawer file cabinet by scanning everything in it into Evernote. What's more, with the programs tag feature, you can identify each document through its tags for multiple purposes. For example, if you write gift annuities for clients, not only would you tag each document with the name of the client, you would also tag them with the type of annuity. That way, if you wanted to find a sample to emulate for another client, it would only be a search algorithm away.

Related, although not specifically for the use of your business purposes, are programs that your clients use to carry out their functions. An entire industry has grown around nonprofit specific back-office programs for fundraising, accounting, memberships, ticketing and other services. Some of these are even mission related, like only working with churches or summer day camps or hospitals or educational institutions. Depending upon the work you do, consider training and becoming an "affiliate" for that software program. As an affiliate, you may be able to recommend a particular piece of software to your client through a discount code that is unique to you. By using that code, the software vendor might provide you with money or some other benefit in thanks.

Exercise 32

Review the software you own and compare it to the above list. Where are the gaps and how can you fill those gaps with inexpensive, pay-as-you-use, or free software solutions?

_____

_____

_____

3 MONEY AND LEGAL

Do you need an attorney?

Kind of. What you need is a relationship with an attorney. That means you should identify someone before you need the service… and you may never need the service. Still, before you say "I'll cross that bridge when I get to it," or worse yet, make that call to a stranger in a panicked sweat, consider that having an attorney friend or two could be excellent for networking and marketing.

Where do you start?

Like was mentioned earlier, your attorney can be a key part of your team. Since small business (which is what you expect to be) is so ubiquitous in our culture, there are more than enough attorneys with small business experience to choose from. Know also that due to the glut of law school graduates, it is a very competitive business. That means that attorneys are likely to advertise, join business associations and keep a good web presence and more, to get your business. There are a few places to start when looking for a small business attorney:

- Your personal network: friends, family and professional connections.

- Your local chamber of commerce.

- Directories, such as Martindale Hubbell (www.martindale.com/Find-Lawyers-and-Law-Firms.aspx) or Nolo. (www.nolo.com/lawyers)

- Your local bar association. (http://apps.americanbar.org/legalservices/lris/directory/)

- Ask other members of your team, like your accountant or insurance broker.

After you identify one or more, start setting appointments. Go into your meeting with some questions in mind, like...

- Does your personality seem to fit with the lawyer in front of you? Are you looking for someone aggressive or cautious? Do you want a negotiator or a winner-take-all approach? Do you want someone to just process paper?

- Does the lawyer communicate well? Was there a follow up to your visit, and how soon? Did their office look organized? Did they have an assistant, and was s/he organized and friendly (because that's who much of your communication will be with).

- Is the attorney taking clients? If s/he is, will you be dealing directly with him or her, or with a junior associate? How many consultants do they serve, and how?

- What is their fee structure? Will you get charged for time not used (does the lawyer have a minimum billing time?) Can you pay a small yearly fee for a retainer service?

- You might even ask if they serve on any nonprofit boards or volunteer in other capacities. It might lead to a client referral.

Exercise 33

Identifying your attorney.

Using the resources named above (and the one, below), identify at least three attorneys in your area who specialize in small business. Name them here:

_____

_____

_____

____ Make appointments with two.

Another way to identify a small business attorney is to ask a nonprofit attorney.

There is a growing subspecialty of attorneys who focus on nonprofit matters. Knowing you and your skills means you can get referrals to their clients and friends, and they can be a resource for your clients. While a nonprofit attorney may not be able to take on a situation where you need legal services because you are a business, not a nonprofit, you now have a source for an excellent referral for your own needs. Of course, you should always consider reciprocating when the opportunity presents itself.

Therefore, put on your task list to identify at least one, if not a handful of attorneys who specialize in nonprofits. Most I know are in small firms, or solo practitioners. However, there are many larger firms with a nonprofit group, or at least lawyers who focus on that area when the firm is in need. Like a business attorney, a good place to start your search is with your local Bar Association (apps.americanbar.org/legalservices/findlegalhelp/home.cfm), or the Martindale Hubbell website (www.martindale.com/Find-Lawyers-and-Law-Firms.aspx). In addition, you can ask around among your nonprofit colleagues or a university nonprofit center. The nice thing is that most nonprofit attorneys I know "get it" when it comes to seeking business, and will sometimes connect emerging consultants to nonprofits, if for nothing else than for the possibility of a future connection to your clients and colleagues. It's a nice symbiosis.

A caution: not to disparage the profession, but even attorney friends of mine will admit to the propensity to say "yes" when asked "can you do…?" in any legal matter. So if you say, "do you work with nonprofits?" they're inclined to say "yes" first, then study up later. Therefore, make sure you connect with attorneys who clearly indicate they work with nonprofits, and better yet, as a primary specialty.

Exercise 34

Using the resources named above and other references, identify attorneys in your area who specialize in nonprofit work. Name them here:

_____

_____

_____

____ Make networking appointments with two.

Should you incorporate?

Incorporation is a good idea if you have something to protect, like your house or other personal significant assets (even a retirement plan). If you incorporate, and your business fails or is sued (justifiably or not), the incorporated business would take the hit, but your personal assets would be protected. It's called the "corporate veil."

Like any good piece of material, if you're going to make that "veil" work for you, you have to keep it up and well maintained. That means filing taxes correctly and on a timely basis, and holding and officially recording annual meetings, and other processes (for more on this, ask your accountant or lawyer). And no, being incorporated is not an excuse to "write off" expenses that are otherwise personal. Some believe that people who own small businesses are more tax audit prone than those who get regular paychecks, so count on the IRS looking into your expenses once in a while. Make sure you can appropriately justify every business expensed cent. Look to your accountant on advice in this area.

You've probably seen television commercials for companies that offer incorporation services, and you may have seen computer programs, too. As you view these, keep in mind the saying "he who acts as his own attorney has a fool for a client." Many attorneys don't charge for an initial visit, so make the call to a few just to explore. S/he will help you decide, among other things, whether you need to incorporate, in what form, and help you file those papers. In addition, s/he might also annually remind you to do what's necessary to keep your incorporation

Remember that your organizational structure is a tool. There is nothing inherently good or bad about any type. It is just a means of accomplishing your objectives.

By way of some review, here are your organizational options.

If you want more details, go here:

http://www.natptax.com/TaxKnowledgeCenter/FederalTaxInformation/Documents/Chart%20of%20Entity%20Comparison.pdf

Easier and less expensive, but more risk:

- Sole proprietor

- Partnership (you should also have a partnership agreement - again, ask an attorney)

Harder and more expensive, but less personal risk are:

- Limited Liability Corporation (LLC)

- Limited Liability Partnership

- S-Corp

For a more detail see the Nolo Series book "LLC or Corporation?: How to Choose the Right Form for Your Business," by Anthony Mancuso.

B-Corp. A "benefit corporation" is a relatively new concept. These are for-profit businesses organized for the public and shareholder's good. Not all states have adopted the form. A good resource is Ryan Honeyman's "The B Corp Handbook: How to Use Business as a Force for Good." Go to https://www.bcorporation.net/ and you'll find a voluntary certification system if you'd rather not incorporate as a B Corp, if your state does not allow it, or if you have already incorporated in another way.

In addition to the above, there is nothing that stops you from being a "C-Corp," (like some of the corporate giants of our time.) Know that C-Corps are typically more expensive and cumbersome in the long run, unless you have really big plans (ask your accountant why).

For that matter, you could also organize as a nonprofit. I know an organization that typically would have been a for-profit business to serve nonprofits, either as an LLC or S-Corp. For philosophical and marketing reasons, the founder selected to become a nonprofit, instead. It's not clear yet whether this was a good move, but it is an option for you.

It is important to remember that however you organize, all corporate types (including nonprofits) are born at the state level, so the laws and fees around how you organize will vary.

Of course, what I offer here is simply an outline. If you want to get more detailed advice on your personal situation, now's the time to find that attorney. (By the way… many accountants will offer to help you with incorporation, too. They see incorporation as a tax matter, and they're right. Visit with one or two and weigh your options.)

After that, you probably don't need an attorney regularly, although I know of exceptions. For example, an acquaintance specializes in writing for nonprofits in a very controversial area. He regularly risks, or puts his clients at risk, for defamation suits. Everything he puts out he sends to his attorney for screening.

Exercise 35

____ Review your business structure (incorporation or not, and if so, how) with your attorney or accountant.

Confidentiality and confidentiality agreements.

Just like the definition of "anonymous" varies from donor to donor, "confidentiality" is defined by your client. I suggest a general rule to be circumspect in your discussion about clients or their issues with just about anyone. That doesn't stop you from talking in general, anonymous, terms about clients or their issues with colleagues and friends. "Hey, Bob, I have a disease organization client who..." is fine, unless for some reason the name of the client is given away in the circumstance you describe.

This differs from promotion. I have a clause in most of my contracts giving the client's express permission to recognize my client publicly as someone I work with. Some don't want that and remove it. That's fine. The point is that if I have their permission, I become their advocate in the community, and in doing so, promote my own business as well. Nearly all clients see the advantage in that.

On some occasions, a client wants me to sign their confidentiality agreement. Usually that's okay. Not one is the same between clients, but most cover some form of:

- Mission recipient contact - Social service and healthcare organizations and a few others are legally and ethically bound to keep their interactions with clients as confidential, and as their consultant, require you to do the same.

- Related to this is when a job entails the use of your client's mission recipients (their clients), volunteers or donors as public examples for some kind of work product, like fundraising solicitation material. Always have your client contact those volunteers, donors or mission recipients before you do. In addition, get the volunteer's, donor's or mission recipient's express permission to use their names or images in the material you produce for them.

- Consider also that you could make up names for your purposes, and get stock photography. I have no problem doing this for privacy purposes, and maintaining the dignity of the mission recipient, as long as the story behind the image or name is true. For children, I am particularly inclined to use made-up names and stock images. These days, I find that nearly everyone understands this concern.

- Organizational records - Your client has a right to keep their records private, like donor, billing and other records and reports.

- Organizational processes - Once in a while I see something that covers "proprietary work product." If it's a process that they have established and you're seeing it? No problem. If it's the work product you produce for them as part of the contract? No problem. The issue comes when they claim that all you do for them to produce that work product, which may include processes you do for others when you produce similar product for earlier or later clients. What I typically find is that this is boilerplate language cribbed from another organization or suggested by their attorney. Consider pushing back, or consult your attorney to see that you have it right. If in the end you can't live with the condition, walk away. The prospective client might call you back and change their mind.

When it comes to confidentiality, privacy and being anonymous, make it a policy to ask your client, and your attorney, if there is any doubt about the document in front of you. This is not an area where you need to get tied up when a minor misunderstanding blows up to something bigger.

Exercise 36

____ Research confidentiality agreements in your discipline. (For example, some disciplines and their professional organizations have template language you could find helpful.)

Fundraising registration

This section is specifically for people who are doing fundraising as their consulting specialty. It's important for you to know that more than 30 states require people who consult with nonprofits for fundraising to register with that state. The requirements for who registers vary widely. Some states require you to register if you touch any aspect of fundraising, including writing grant proposals, solicitation letters and case statements. Other states draw the circle very tightly, and only include direct fundraising advising. Many states divide the types of consultants into "fundraising counsel" versus "fundraising solicitors." Definitions of these vary.

In states that have registration, what they all have in common is that you must register in the state in which your client is based. There is no reciprocity between states, nor is your registration transferable. For example, as a Pennsylvania registered fundraising counsel, I cannot work for a New Jersey based client without registering there. On the other hand, I can work in Delaware because they have no registration system (as of this writing).

Registration will often cost money (the biggest I am aware of is New York, for $800) and typically requires you to mail your contract with the nonprofit to a state agency for final approval. Of course, forms are involved. Plus, some states require additional payments for submitting contracts and other transactions.

Adding to the mix, the states among themselves are not consistent with what department handles the registration process. It is typical for the same office to handle fundraiser registration as handles nonprofit charitable gift solicitation registration. These might be in the state's office of attorney general, the secretary of state, or, for at least one state I know of, the Department of Agriculture (I think, historically, this was based on fundraising auctions.)

For a nice summary of where you need to register, go here: GivingUSA's Annual Survey of State Laws Regulating Charitable Solicitations ($19.95)

http://givingusa.org/product/giving-usa-2015-spotlight-annual-survey-of-state-laws-regulating-charitable-solicitations-as-of-january-1-2015/

Exercise 37

If you plan working as a fundraising consultant, investigate the laws in your state and other states where you could imagine doing business. Summarize your costs, criteria to register and business and/or contract requirements here:

_____

_____

_____

_____

_____

_____

Selecting an accountant

Right up there with thinking you may not need a lawyer, resist the temptation to save money by going without an accountant. Think carefully about this choice. Up to now, as a paycheck employee, you've downloaded your favorite tax program, or walked into the nationally known tax preparer office, and not long later you're filed and done. Once you introduce 1099 income (income where you are paid without taxes withheld via an employer's W-2 process), things start getting complicated. Suddenly you're in the realm of estimated and quarterly tax payments. You will owe state and local taxes, too. On the positive side, you may have certain deductions available to you.

Engaging a local accountant or enrolled agent (a non-CPA tax preparer) has quite a number of advantages for nonprofit consultants. What is an Enrolled Agent?

"An enrolled agent is a person who has earned the privilege of representing taxpayers before the Internal Revenue Service by either passing a three-part comprehensive IRS test covering individual and business tax returns, or through experience as a former IRS employee. Enrolled agent status is the highest credential the IRS awards. Individuals who obtain this elite status must adhere to ethical standards and complete 72 hours of continuing education courses every three years.

"Enrolled agents, like attorneys and certified public accountants (CPAs), have unlimited practice rights. This means they are unrestricted as to which taxpayers they can represent, what types of tax matters they can handle, and which IRS offices they can represent clients before."

(https://www.irs.gov/tax-professionals/enrolled-agents/enrolled-agent-information)

Unless you're seeing one of the big tax national preparers, there's a good chance that you are having your taxes done by a fellow small business person. That means that just like with your attorney, you can build a relationship that leads to both of you getting more business. My guess is that your CPA has a business built on referrals. Help each other out.

A close relationship with your own accountant means they know your situation. You might say "who knows my situation better than me?" Of course, but unless your work is focused on taxes, you probably can't evaluate your financial situation as well as an accountant can.

Also, you can enlist your accountant to help a client. If you do any amount of work with nonprofits, sooner or later someone is going ask you whether you know a CPA. Maybe it's for reviewing the books - pro-bono or for a fee - for the organization. It could also be to join their board. For those reasons and more, having a name or two "in your back pocket" builds your reputation as a resource for your client.

How do you find a CPA or an Enrolled Agent? Like anything personal service, like a lawyer or doctor, identifying someone is easier than finding the right one for you. You have some options in the age of the internet.

Exercise 38

Use the following resources to identify an accountant for your business:

- Your local chamber of commerce. If they're a member, he or she is probably looking for business.

- Fellow consultants. Ask around with a few emails.

- LinkedIn. See who's in your network.

List five you identified:

_____

_____

_____

_____

_____

____ Make networking appointments with two.

Contact and interview, just like you would a new employee hire.

- How do they keep their records secure?

- Do their clients use a particular computer program (QuickBooks, Freshbooks, etc.)?

- Do they have other clients similar to you?

- If you get audited, what's their process and rates.

- Do they use seasonal subcontractors, or does the accountant do all their work his/herself?

- How do you contact them during the "off (tax) season"? (May 1 to December 31)

- How do you contact them during the tax season? (January 1 to April 15)

And above all else, ask yourself "can I get along with her/him?" And don't forget his or her assistant. You'll likely have more contact with him or her than your accountant. Are they friendly, or an obstacle? Does the assistant look organized?

Get references. If you got the name through a connection, ask that person why they like this accountant and if they've worked with her/him.

Know also that some accountants offer financial planning and investment services. You might find this convenient. You might find it invasive. Like the process above, investigate before you buy.

Selecting a bank

Among the "big three" of your professional advisers. You might think that a banker would be the easiest. Maybe… maybe not.

If you're of a certain age, you might remember when bankers were rocks in your community. The people at the bank were there for years. They knew everyone who came in. Personal service came with a smile – and along with that smile, solid advice on achieving your dreams.

Today, with ATMs, direct deposit, and scanning checks with smartphones, you might walk into a bank once a year, if that (and sorry, drive-up windows don't count.) If you do, you'll notice that personnel change regularly. Having them recognize you is very unlikely.

Does that matter? That's up to you. If you plan on using your bank as a holding tank for your money, then maybe automation is fine. If you imagine yourself looking for more advanced services, like a variety of loan products, then a more personal relationship might be key. If that's the case, consider a smaller community bank, or a credit union (a type of nonprofit, by the way – a 501(c)14).

How about using the bank you already use for personal accounts? When I first entered business, I was warned against it. The reasoning went something like "separate your personal and business life in all ways." As I spoke to bankers and accountants, it was clear that this wasn't as much of a concern. Know, however, that banking regulations prohibit you from easily transferring moneys from a personal to a business account and back. So the convenience of staying with your personal bank may only be in driving up to the same window for both business and personal transactions.

Where ever you bank, if you set up a business account, know that you will likely be offered a business credit card, too. Unless you plan to designate a specific personal card for business purchases, having a credit card for your business could be helpful – if only so you can track expenses more easily. You can also build a credit score that could help you get a small loan, if its needed. It's worth considering, especially if it makes your life easier.

Exercise 39

Consider your possible business banking needs. Do you need:

____ Checks to pay vendors?

____ A debit card for incidental expenses?

____ Credit card for paying vendors, or for supplies?

____ Loan(s) for larger expenses?

____ Smart phone app for transactions?

____ Online access for balance checks and transfers?

____ Branch/store locations where you live, travel or have clients?

____ Other features (like international transactions?)

_____

_____

Exercise 40

Do you prefer a...

___ Small community bank or credit union?

___ A bigger bank?

___ Your current, personal bank?

Exercise 41

If you are looking for a bank other than your current bank, list three to investigate, and why:

_____

_____

_____

_____

_____

_____

Your personal budget

Regardless of who you engage as an accountant or bank, developing your own, personal or family spending plan is just good financial sense. Before you start consulting, whether you are doing it full-time as your sole livelihood, or "on-the-side" after work or anything in-between, it is important to know what you need to make so you can live the lifestyle you choose. Even if you are not going to depend upon consulting, it's good to know how your income will fit into your broader household expenses.

Yes, I know it's a task that's only topped on your "fun" list by a very uncomfortable medical procedure. Yes, I know that it means dragging out your checkbook, receipts, bills and other records you'd rather forget about once the information is passed. Still, without having an idea of what you need, you could go blithely (and emotionally) into a situation that you could regret.... And it doesn't have to be that way.

Household budget templates are easily found, whether it's an Excel spreadsheet or part of a more sophisticated program like Quicken (the data from which can convert to QuickBooks, someday.) Your numbers don't need to be to-the-penny exact. Just enough to give you a good idea of your spending habits and if you see any opportunities to trim, if needed. My suggestion is to make this a family exercise, not just your toiling at the kitchen table after everyone else is in bed. That promotes ownership of the numbers, and your new venture.

Don't forget any new expenses as you develop your budget. For example, if you're moving from a paycheck job to full-time consulting, your health insurance situation may change. Factor that in. Also, consider how you will use your car differently. Your accountant can give you some advice here, as well as your insurance agent.

Exercise 42

____ Find a budget template. Consider the Microsoft Suite templates (https://templates.office.com/), one found in a household expense program, such as Quicken (https://www.quicken.com/), or another source.

____ Complete a household budget.

Your consulting budget.

Similarly, you'll need a consulting budget. If you are starting out, all your numbers are going to be speculation. That's okay. It's important to start somewhere.

You might find that many of your initial budget needs are already addressed in what you currently own. You probably have your own computer of some sort, you might have a smartphone already, and even the office supplies could be in a cabinet that you use for paying your personal bills. That's a nice head start. Know that just about everything you have will need replacement at some point or another. For example, you might think you have a nice desk, but you haven't sat at it for hours at a time. It was good when you needed to write a note or pay a few bills, but not when you have a 30-page report to get out next week to a client.

SCORE (which used to stand for "Service Corps of Retired Executives") is a nonprofit, nationwide, business assistance organization. They have an excellent resource site for business planning templates. (https://www.score.org/resource/business-planning-financial-statements-template-gallery)

Exercise 43

____ Complete the Start-Up Expenses worksheet on the SCORE website. (https://www.score.org/resource/start-expenses)

Exercise 44

___ Look for other SCORE templates you will find helpful

Thriftiness.

Thriftiness is great practice for consulting. Now, every dollar you save in your business goes to your own grocery bill, your bathroom renovation or your child's college fund, or whatever you want.

You learn thriftiness early in your career. You wince at spending 50 cents when you think something can be had at 45. You'll put up with 20-year-old paint of it means one more meal to a client. New costumes for the play? Can't we re-tailor last years?

This is great training for consulting. Particularly at the beginning of your practice, it's important to keep your expenses down to maximize your income. One overlooked place to do this is your local thrift store. I found that the right thrift store is a whole lot more than used clothing. Many have excellent opportunities for office supplies, desks, cabinets, and other, smaller office hardware (like hole punchers, for example.) The only problem with a thrift store is that the inventory is rarely consistent. Therefore, you need to take a tour through every few weeks to find what you want. One of the nice things about thrifts is that most are connected in some way to nonprofit organizations who use the donation and sale of secondhand goods as a means of funding their mission. Even for-profit thrift stores buy a substantial part of their inventory from nonprofits. As a person who serves nonprofits, I find this important.

Exercise 45

___ Identify and visit two local thrift stores who have office materials.

Reserve funds.

Taxes, health accounts, short term reserve, long term reserve and retirement. One of the biggest advantages of a paycheck job is the (relative) ease in which you can set aside funds for any number of purposes. A simple form signed at the HR or payroll office can set aside pre-paycheck funds for any number of purposes, like additional retirement dollars, health savings accounts, charitable gifts or simply good ol' savings. You can "set it and forget it" and live off the rest, albeit at a slight lower standard of living.

While this is perfectly possible in consulting, when you're behind payroll to yourself, and your rent or mortgage is due and you didn't get that client you expected last month and you're not sure about next month… it's easy to skip saving until "things get better." When things actually get better, you need to pay this month's new bills, and pay off the credit card you drew from because of last month's shortfall. And don't you deserve a reward for doing well? Of course! Off to dinner you go! Oh… then there's the less immediate, boring, not-immediately gratifying saving for vacation, health care, retirement, reserve funds, and etc. You do put away for taxes, because you know that not paying quarterlies could be massive trouble down the line.

One way to fight this problem is not to get into it in the first place. Since having an emergency fund of 3 months' expenses is good financial management anyway, starting your consulting career "on the side," could be a way to building that account. If you're starting after being laid off and it comes with any kind of severance, then a portion of that can get you started.

If you're jumping in full-time, then it might take longer to build. Either way, it will take discipline.

One thing's for certain, when you start into consulting, there's uncertainty. Part time or full-time, in any discipline, unless you have a regularly paying ongoing client (and that sounds like a job, not a client), you are going to have variable income over the period of a year.

Therefore, being able to juggle your finances is a very useful skill, and building an emergency fund is important.

Exercise 46

____ Discuss reserve funds with your account and/or financial advisor.

Exercise 47

____ Begin a reserve/emergency fund. Determine a small amount you can lay aside monthly.

How do you get paid?

Chances are that you're coming to consulting from a "paycheck job." Most people do. Whether you get paid biweekly, semimonthly, or monthly, you see a regular paycheck with deductions like Social Security, healthcare, taxes and other requirements or options you chose.

It is possible that either you will land a job with a consulting firm that will continue this tradition in your life, or work for a client who would like to put you on the payroll as a part-time employee. If this happens, you are likely spending a substantial amount of time with that client, or the client has policies that prohibit it from bringing on independent contractors. Receiving a regular paycheck from a client is not a problem. In fact, it could make your life easier when it comes to tax time. In the language of the American employment paradigm, you are known as a "W-2" worker.

It is more likely that you will enter into what the IRS calls a "contractor" relationship with your client. The IRS is very careful to define this, and I encourage you to look up the "IRS 20 factor test" as you move ahead with your consulting. Knowing the requirements for a contractor versus the employee will help clarify your relationship with your client. The common HR/finance phrase for your status is a "1099" worker (named after the form which you are mailed by your clients at year's end for tax purposes.) As a contractor, you will need to fill out a W-9 on an annual basis for each client. This is a simple form which is downloadable through the IRS website. My suggestion is to do one early in the year and scan it. This way you can simply email it to every client at the start or end of your contracting process. (https://www.irs.gov/pub/irs-pdf/fw9.pdf)

By way of a reminder, as a 1099 worker, you will not have any taxes taken out, benefits addressed, or other deductions from the payment you receive from a client. It will be purely the amount you bill. You will be responsible for any taxes. Make sure you look up your state's and municipality's regulations for quarterly tax payments, plus the federal government's requirements for the same. All of these organizations tend to get grumpy (and worse) if you either neglect quarterly payments or paying at all. See your accountant for more on this.

Exercise 48

___ Download, sign, scan and store this year's W-9 in your computer, in a place you can easily find, so you can send to clients as needed.

Payment Types:

Once you've sent your invoice, you have some choices on your preferred method of payment, dependent upon the processes of your client. Although a bit old fashioned, most organizations will send you a check through the postal mail. I have to confess that it's still nice to get money in the mail amongst any bills I still get that way, or the junk mail I received.

You also have other choices. I have one client who requires their departments to use credit cards for payment. I already had a PayPal account, so I set it up for receiving funds from that client. If credit cards become a frequent option of choice for you or your clients, it's worth investigating providers that will charge you a low rate depending on your volume. Another way of getting paid is through a direct transfer of funds from your client's account to yours. This is not common but may be an option if you want to avoid working through a credit card processing company.

Exercise 49

____ Develop a template invoice by developing your own, finding one in the template section on MS Office (https://templates.office.com/), or through a business accounting program, such as QuickBooks (https://quickbooks.intuit.com/) or Freshbooks (https://www.freshbooks.com/)

Exercise 50

____ Investigate opening a PayPal or other credit card receiving account where you can take funds.

Setting your price.

Asking someone what he or she charges to clients is probably the most sensitive question I've run into in any conversation with a fellow consultant. The problem is that it is too easy to undercut your competition, and there are too many variables involved in the calculation. So while I would encourage you to ask your fellow consultants, be ready for some obfuscation on the topic. Here's some factors to consider in setting your price:

> ● **Your experience.** Intuitively, it makes sense that the more experience you come with, the higher you're able to charge because with experience comes value. However, is not always the case. Less experienced competitors who market better than you could appear to bring more value to clients, or you don't state the value you bring in terms that the client understands, or cares about.

> ● **What the client will bear.** Ideally, you want to charge the maximum your client is willing to pay. Too much, and you don't get the job. Too little, and you leave money behind. Maybe the only way to do this is to come in a bit high, then negotiate down. However, that only works if the client really wants your services. Otherwise, if you come in too high, they won't even bother asking you to revisit your quote. It's a delicate balance that causes stress to consultants on an ongoing basis.

> ● **What you need.** This is more a factor in your flexibility than in your final number. If you need less because, for instance, your income is a supplement to someone else's in the household, you can opt to charge less if necessary. If you are the primary income generator, you have a higher minimum rate. The bad news is that your requirements may take you out of contention for a lot of jobs you might think are interesting or fun, or where you see the nonprofit's need. The good news is that, as you'll see below, it makes you appear more valuable, since (for better or worse) people tend to equate higher price, thus exclusivity, with higher quality.

> ● **Your self-confidence.** You will be surprised what this does to your ability to charge.

If you feel valuable, you transmit that in all you do, and feel more confident in charging more. This is hardest in the beginning, and especially as it impacts pricing your services. It is easy to fall into the trap of "giving it all away" as you sell yourself to a client. You tell yourself that you are trying to prove to your client that you know what you're doing. Maybe that's true, in part. But what you're also doing (unconsciously?) is building your self-confidence, and proving to yourself that you are worth paying based on their reaction to the value you bring. It also shoots you in the foot. As nonprofits, too many organizations are more than happy to have you volunteer your expertise, intentionally or not.

● **Your market "position."** This is probably the most overlooked factor in pricing. Here's a true story that just happened in my home town.

I read on a Facebook group that a local, high end bakery just closed. The owner, in her frustration, lashed out at some people in the group who were surprised to find the doors locked. It was clear that her customers did not perceive her wares as "high end." They said that they usually got their cakes at local groceries. Not to disparage those that posted, but my guess is that they really didn't know what a better cake tasted like, or if they did, didn't value it for their purposes (myself included). It didn't help that the bakery was not easy to see from the street, and in the least attractive shopping center in town, anchored by a not-well-kept discount store, a hardware store, and next to a liquor store and a bar. Maybe the rent was all she thought she could afford starting out? Regardless, her inability to make the perception of her product worth the higher price she was charging, added to where she selected as a location was a recipe (sorry!) for failure. Her actual baking acumen had little to do with her success or failure. For the clientele she was attracting due to the location, her pricing was seen as "expensive" and "unaffordable," not "quality." If she had been in an easily seen location in the "village" part of town, and cultivated relationships with people who valued quality baked goods and were willing to pay for them, she may have had a shot.

Ask yourself, "How am I perceived by potential customers?" While your location is probably not a factor like a bakery's, what's your "location" in terms of what events you attend and clients you serve? Does your messaging and pricing help prospects perceive your work as quality? Does your website look modern and quality? Are you easy to contact? Are you easy to work with? Do people speak highly of your work?

Pricing as marketing: Quality and Value.

We're a bit ahead of ourselves here (because marketing comes later in this book), but you should consider your pricing is a key part of your marketing strategy. Like we noted above, people equate price with quality. Quality is a standard of "good" they think you will deliver. If you're really "good" at what you do - often a function of level of activity, not necessarily amount of activity - you deliver higher quality. When your client weighs the amount of "good" against the amount of money you charge for that "good," they perceive "value." While quality is important, "value," in my opinion, is the gold standard. I find most clients expect high quality, and they say they want it at as low a price as they can find it. However, what someone says and what they do are often very different. Let's look at this a bit mathematically:

Given that: Value = Price / Quality. Therefore:

- (High Price/Low Quality = Poor Value) You don't want to be here. You may get a few clients, but soon enough you'll get a reputation that will end, or significantly retard, your business.

- (Low Price/High Quality = Very High Value) This is great for your client, but not so much for you. While you might say "I want to offer my client as much as possible for their money," you need to be able to eat while you do it. Plus, over time, you may feel your clients are taking advantage of you (because you're letting them) and end up resenting them. That will erode your quality of work.

- (Low Price/Low Quality = Some Value) A lot of huge retailers take this strategy. As long as you know that you are not getting the best, but what you need, no problem. So it should be with your clients. If they're on board with paying less but getting less, and it will solve their problem, then go for it. After all, if you're just going a few blocks, do you need the super SUV with mag wheels and the most comfortable seats, or can you just ride your "beater bike?" Know, however, that doing this too much will give you a reputation for low quality work.

- (High Price/High Quality = Solid Value) In my opinion, this is where you want to be. You want to be paid enough so that you feel good offering high quality work. This builds a positive reputation. People will recommend you saying "it may cost a bit more, but you'll get results." You will go into clients with enthusiasm for your work. They will sense that and feel like they're getting more. It's a win/win.

So what equals a high price, or a low price? Let's step back and look at an event you were recently asked to attend. Maybe it's a seminar on a topic you know would be good for your ability to bring in more clients. Now the event is upon you, and you're thinking how tired you are after a whole day with your client. You're thinking "should I go?"

If the seminar were free, you might blow it off, relax at home and enjoy something in TV. Yes, you know it can help your business, "but," you ask yourself, "if it's free, how valuable could it be?"

Now ask "What price level would make me wince if I missed that seminar?" Five dollars? Ten? Twenty-five? Whatever that number is, that's the seminar's minimum price to charge each person to get them to actually attend. Yes, you heard that right. "Free," while attention getting, is not a price to get people to attend something. Instead, set a price that they can commit to, but feel a loss if they do not attend. Even at that price, you'll get some no-shows. So for those no-shows, the price wasn't high enough.

On the other end, when you received the invitation, ask yourself "what's the price where I would simply say 'no-can-do,' regardless of the value the seminar brings you?" That's the price above which the presenter has not made his value proposition compelling enough for you to pay more. Just below that number is the maximum the host can charge you for that seminar. Notice that I said "the maximum they can charge _you_." That's _your_ maximum. Someone else could have a lower, or higher maximum.

If your goal is to get lots of people to your event (or get lots of clients for your service), then you'll charge in the low range of this bracket. However, for each client, you won't make as much for what might be the same amount of work. If your objective is to have fewer, but higher paying attendees (clients), you charge closer to the top. You'll make more per attendee (client). The effort to put on the seminar is the same either way.

Price push back? Change what you do, not how much you do it for.

A lot of businesses will tell you that nonprofits are notorious for "pleading poor" when it comes to vendors. There's some truth to that. Sometime, I guarantee, you'll hear "I don't have the budget for your services." That may be true, but you and I know that "having the budget" is not the same as "having the money." If a prospective client really wants your service, budgets can change as long as the cash is there. Budgets equal priorities.

That said, sooner-or-later you'll be asked to come in with a lower price. Be cautious. Just cutting your prices for the exact same work sends a message that you were inflating your price in the first place. That erodes trust. Instead, adjust the nature or volume of the work. If you quote $2,500 to research, write and follow up on a grant proposal, and you're asked whether you can do it for $1,000, reply "for that much, I can write the grant if you provide the research and follow up." Unless you have a real passion for the mission (and at that rate, maybe you should volunteer?), think hard about simply discounting your work. People like to brag about bargains, and pretty soon you'll have the reputation of the one who will lower prices. Your quotes will become meaningless, and when you don't lower your price for someone, they'll resent it because you lowered your price for their friend.

When should you give a discount? Watch your business cycle. You might offer a "sale" when you're typically down. For example, maybe December is slow because your clients are distracted by year-end fundraising? That may be the perfect time to offer a lower price to fill your schedule, and bring in cash when you had none before. Just make sure that everyone knows that this is a "limited time offer." You can offer this deal to long-time clients who you like to work with, enabling them to "bank" some material for future use, or as an incentive for new customers to try your services (be careful... unless you're clear that this is a special event, new customers may expect this lower price all of the time.)

Exercise 51

Which half-months will be slow due to the nature of your particular work? Circle them below:

Early Jan	Early Apr	Early Jul	Early Oct
Late Jan	Late Apr	Late Jul	Late Oct
Early Feb	Early May	Early Aug	Early Nov
Late Feb	Late May	Late Aug	Late Nov
Early Mar	Early Jun	Early Sep	Early Dec
Late Mar	Late Jun	Late Sep	Late Dec

What if you mess up?

Hey, it's going to happen. You'll miss a deadline. You'll misinterpret the client's instructions. You'll forget about some aspect of a project because you were focusing too much on the other parts. It's easy to do.

First of all, relax. We've all been there. Step back and ask yourself why it happened. Do you have too much work load? Were the instruction not clear? Did you not ask for clarification when you had a question? Do you need to be better organized? Did you promise too much in too short a time? Is this a subliminal, passive way to punish your client for being difficult to work with? Did your client change the conditions of the work in the middle of the project?

Why you messed up is important… to a point. If it is clear that for some reason you didn't take the right steps, either because of your own disorganization, over-promising in time or work product, or from an uncontrollable life event on your part (sudden serious illness in the family that required your attention, for example), then you should consider reducing your price as a good-will gesture toward your client. You may or may not get that client back after the job is done. It could also boost your professional reputation. Your client might sing your praises for being so flexible, and not even mention the issue that caused it.

What if it's your client's fault? For example, what if your work-product requires a series of interviews with staff or board members? If you did your level best to schedule them within the agreed upon time table and some were not possible to meet, make note of it in your report, and let your client contact know as it happens (not at the end of the project.) Like personnel issues back in your paycheck days, client issues that prevent completion or cause delay in a project must be documented. Your client contact can address the issue internally, and you don't need to feel like you should bill for less than the full amount quoted.

Deposits

A lot of consultants will ask for a portion of their fee as a "deposit" before they get started on a project. It might be half up-front and half on completion, or a one-third at the start, one-third at some sort or a benchmark and the last third at conclusion. Some will look for monthly payments.

Why do this? If you have material to buy, time to reserve with a vendor, or other immediate expense you can project, then this can provide you with the up-front funds to move ahead with the project. It's like a carpenter wanting half up-front to start work on your deck. Some of that money could be used to buy supplies.

If you're dealing with a new nonprofit, or a client with whom you have not worked before, whether you have expenses or not, getting a deposit will assure you that even if the worst goes wrong – like not paying you at the end – you will get something for the job.

On the other hand, if they're an established client, or the job has a very low price, or if their internal systems make getting a deposit difficult, or you simply don't want the hassle of billing, then assess your risk and don't ask for the partial payment.

Whichever you do, make sure that you clarify the arrangement in your contract so there are no surprises on either of your parts.

Client payment plans and schedules

Agreeing to how much to get paid, and when to get paid, are different concepts. Like any organization, whether business or nonprofit, there are times of year when cash flow is better than others. In addition, many of your clients will feel better making final payments after the work is complete. This makes defining "complete" a very important contract provision. Is it your delivery date? Their final approval date? Publication? Your last day of work?

How long will it be before you see a check? It depends. Some of my smallest clients pay immediately, and the biggest lag and lag, and the other way around too. It could be that your contact person has little control over the payment system beyond filling out a payment request form. If you work long enough with a client, you'll be able to plan for their payment patterns. You could also handle credit cards, which makes life easier for you and your client – assuming you are okay with the fee charge to you, and the client has a card to use.

Purchase Orders ("PO")

Some clients, usually the bigger and more sophisticated ones, will require a purchase order to pay any bill over whatever threshold they determine internally (like $5,000, for example.)

What is a purchase order? Our friends at Wikipedia quote Dobler, Donald W; Burt, David N (1996). Purchasing and Supply Management, Text and Cases (Sixth ed.). Singapore: McGraw-Hill. p. 70. (https://en.wikipedia.org/wiki/Purchase_order):

"A purchase order (PO) is a commercial document and first official offer issued by a buyer to a seller, indicating types, quantities, and agreed prices for products or services. It is used to control the purchasing of products and services from external suppliers.

What's this mean to you? If you're working with a bigger organization, ask your client contact whether the organization issues you a purchase order to initiate payment for your services. If so, the next question should be "is there something I can do to help move the process forward?" You might be required to provide certain paperwork, or simply a copy of a projected invoice. Then, the client (or more typically, their accounting office) will send you the purchase order. You return it with your official invoice, thus triggering payment. Not following their process may cause significant delay in your payment.

Your biggest competitor?

You might think that the consultant down the street or across the country is your biggest competitor, especially when it comes to price. You would be wrong. Regardless of how much you charge or what value you bring, the old sales saying maybe most true when working with nonprofits: Your client is your biggest competitor. Why? Volunteers.

More than once, I was told "we got a volunteer to do it." In a world of "fast, good or cheap, pick two," they chose "cheap" and are trying to figure which of other one out the remaining two they can get. Will it be quality work? Will it be timely work? They may not even get two. The perception of saving money won. Perception? Well, you know like I do, that even if the expense didn't show up on their books, a nonprofit could still lose money in unrealized revenue or incurred expenses by not acting in a timely manner.

I know a lot of consultants who say, with some justified pique, "you can't compete against free." Yeah, they're right. It's not fair or kind, especially when they just took your valuable time pumping you for information for a job they never intended to use you for. My advice? Walk away and don't worry about those clients - hard as it may be. You won't be able to sway them, and you need to put your energy elsewhere - like into prospects who see the value of your services.

How do I charge?

Far and above all others, the most popular question I get from new consultants is "how much do I charge?" Sorry, the answer is "it depends." Given the above, your first steps start with methodology, not amount. Basically, you have three methods of charging clients.

- By the hour.

- By the job.

- By commission.

As you would expect, each comes with pros and cons. Let's take a look.

By the hour. This is by far the most popular way to charge clients.

The positives:

- You get what you work. You work five hours; you get paid for five hours.

- Your clients understand it. Hourly wages are a standard in our culture.

- You can more easily estimate your income.

- You get to charge more when your client makes changes - especially important in design and writing jobs, but others, too.

- You don't get stuck (or at least less often) with doing work that you can't bill for.

The negatives:

- It's hard to track your time.

- You only have so much time in a day

- You may grossly miss your estimated hours. This will make for a very unhappy client.

- Setting your rate can be complicated (more on this, below).

- Your client is cautious about your time on the job.

- You'll probably never bill a 40-hour week.

- Your client simply wants the job done, and wishes you'd spend less time doing it.

- You focus on your hours, not our product.

- Your tempted to pad hours (Resist this temptation. It is fraud!).

- It is unfair to your client. Not all tasks are worth the same rate per hour.

- Your client may not like it if you "learn on my time."

- You short yourself by inaccurate counting or being "nice" (or less confident.)

The simplest way to calculate your hourly fee is to double or triple what you make (or made) per hour at your paycheck job. Why two or three times as much? Because you probably won't be billing the hours that you worked at your job. Marketing and back-office work may take as much as two-thirds of your time, especially at the start. Also, don't forget to add in the amount your employer paid in benefits and taxes (if you don't know, add about ⅓ more). Also, reduce your time by the number of hours (weeks) of vacation you want.

However, you may want to get more sophisticated. Let's look at another way.

Line	Explanation	Calculation
A	Weekdays in a year:	260
B	Number of holidays you want:	20
C	Number of sick days you want:	5
D	Number work days (Line A - (Line B + Line C))	235
E	Percent of Non-Client work time (Admin, Marketing, etc.)	50%
F	Billable Client days (Line D x Line E)	117.5
G	Convert days to hours (Line F x 8 hours/day)	940
H	Amount of salary you want to make (if based on your paycheck job, include benefits)	$75,000.00
I	Base hourly rate = Line H/Line G	$79.79
J	Annual overhead expenses (paper, toner, phone, technology, etc. - this number is a guess for this calculation)	$5,000.00
K	Annual overhead per hour (Line J/Line G)	$5.32
L	Revised Hourly (Line J + Line I)	$85.11
M	Account for bad debts (add what percent you think you will have in unpaid billings: 5%? So Line L x 1.05)	$89.36
N	Add profit margin (since this is a business, not a paycheck, add profit to your business. 10 to 30%. For our example, 10%)	$98.30
O	Final Number, Round to the nearest 5	$100.00

At this point, the question is does that bottom number fit into the market you're trying to serve? You'll only find out in time, as you propose jobs and talk with other consultants (who may or may not tell you if you're out of range.)

Exercise 52

Calculate your hourly rate:

Line	Explanation	Calculation
A	Weekdays in a year:	
B	Number of holidays you want:	
C	Number of sick days you want:	
D	Number work days (Line A - (Line B+Line C))	
E	Percent of Non-Client work time (Admin, Marketing, etc.)	
F	Billable Client days (Line D x Line E)	
G	Convert days to hours (Line F x 8 hours/day)	
H	Amount of salary you want to make (if based on your paycheck job, include benefits)	
I	Base hourly rate = Line H/Line G	
J	Annual overhead expenses (paper, toner, phone, technology, etc. - this number is a guess for this calculation)	
K	Annual overhead per hour (Line K/Line G)	
L	Revised Hourly (Line J + Line I)	
M	Account for bad debts (add what percent you think you will have in unpaid billings: 5%? So Line L x 1.05)	
N	Add profit margin (since this is a business, not a paycheck, add profit to your business. 10 to 30%. For our example, 10%)	
O	Final Number, Round to the nearest 5	

By the job (also known as "project based" or "flat fee.")

The positives:

- Your clients will like the stability for their budget.

- No tracking hours/minutes on a job.

- Your fee is not limited by the time you put into the job, especially if you're quick to complete the work.

- You have an unlimited "upside" because the more you get done, the more you get paid.

- You will not be charging "learning time" to clients for work you're not familiar with.

- As you get better at doing something, it will take you less time, so your effective hourly rate increases.

The negatives:

- Projects can be difficult to estimate.

- At the start, you may not be as efficient as you will be someday in the future. It will be easy to underestimate the time required on a job.

- You may be reluctant to charge more for client add-ons.

- Your quality of work may suffer as you try to speed through a project.

- Client may not perceive value if you work too quickly.

When I started charging by the job, I usually calculated my total estimated hourly fee for a project and just gave that number, hoping that I wouldn't be too far off. As I got better at it, I could figure out the right fee without the calculations. Today, I also have "standard pricing" for particular job types that came up frequently.

Exercise 53

Consider your two most common jobs. Calculate and compare your hourly rate and flat fee rate for each job.

Job:	Hours	Hourly Rate Total	Estimated Flat Fee

Commissions

As someone who comes out of a fundraising tradition, I look very dimly on commissions when dealing with nonprofit organizations. Yes, according to the Association of Fundraising Professionals Code of Ethics, commissions are not allowed. That's simply codifying what is a very good idea for both the consultants and the nonprofit you serve. Let me enumerate some reasons:

- Commissions put the consultant's profit ahead of the nonprofit's mission. Unique to nonprofits is the mission orientation. It's the core of everything they do. Once a commission is introduced, the question becomes in the minds of many, "are you doing this for the mission, or your commission?" You want to put yourself on the same side as your clients, which means that you want to help them work toward their mission.

- Aligned with this, commissions erode trust. Certainly in a donor environment, but also with others, people will question your motivation once they find out that you are earning a commission.

- Commissions are shortsighted. Yes, nonprofits need to make their budget numbers like anybody else. But when given the choice between a short-term, commission based transaction and a long-term, relationship-based interaction, it is almost always best for the nonprofit to look long-term for its success.

- Commissions leave others uncompensated. Whether it is the secretary who pulled together the proposal or the person right before you who set up the deal, when a nonprofit pays based on commission, your commission does not recognize other's contribution to the effort. You might say "who cares?" You'll find that nonprofits are often much more democratic in their culture than the business community. By leaving people who worked uncompensated, you can easily erode the morale of the organization.

- Commissions might be illegal. This is worth checking out in your state. Particularly for fundraising, some states prohibit commissions. Investigate before you proceed.

The above said, some consulting is traditionally based on commission. For example, I know people who work with energy savings programs or help combine equipment, such as copiers and faxes and scanners, who receive commissions for the money they save an organization. If your business model is established on this kind of basis, simply make sure that you are clear with the nonprofit for where your payments come from.

Exercise 54

____ Check with state agencies and/or professional association in your discipline about their stance on commissions when working with nonprofits.

Responding to RFPs

Getting invited to respond to an "RFP," Request for Proposal, sounds like a gift from heaven to many a newly starting consultant. "Hey, I'm getting a shot!" you say to yourself. Well, you are, kind of.

For a nonprofit, an RFP is an exercise in due diligence. The client is, in effect, bidding out their project and naming the conditions for the bids. It's like they are asking for grant proposals. If they get similar information from everyone, they can best compare the vendor's quality and price (and therefore, value). To them, it also takes the politics out of the process, so board member Josie's best buddy Bob doesn't get the job because he's Josie's favorite.

Shouldn't we all be for fairness and against favoritism? For you, the consultant, it's not that simple.

Experienced consultants are very cautious about RFPs. I know some who won't even respond. Why?

- RFP responses take time. A lot of RFPs ask for a volume of information in a format you don't usually maintain. It's just time consuming to pull it all together.

- RFPs can be complicated. A lot of RFPs can make your taxes seem easy and straightforward.

- RFPs turn you into a commodity. Implicit in an RFP is that your service is interchangeable with whoever else received the RFP. That's true, to a point, but you probably offer unique aspects to your work that would not express well simply on paper.

- RFP remove relationships. If what you do depends on building relationships, then an RFP where you boil your work down to cold numbers is not a good way to start.

- RFPs reduce your chance of getting a job. Whether this is perception or reality is hard to say. But if you're one of ten receiving the RFP, you have a 10% chance of getting the job at the start. If five respond, you're only up to 20%. That's still not great odds.

Should you not reply to an RFP? It's up to you. Go ahead if you think it will lead to something. Just go in with your eyes open.

Because RFPs vary so much in their requirements, I don't know that I can provide an exercise for this one. Just judge the amount of information required, your ability to meet the requirements easily, and whether the time (and the odds) of your getting selected by the nonprofit are favorable enough for you to apply. If you have any questions, call the nonprofit. Like grant proposals, some nonprofits will welcome your inquiries, and others will not.

Contracts: you can't live with 'em, you can't live without 'em.

Back in my fundraising paycheck life, I had a major real estate developer as a client. On one visit, I caught him right after a protracted negotiation for a significant project. He said (to paraphrase) ...

"Contracts are funny things. If everything's going great, nobody cares about the contract. When things are bad, everyone hates the contract! Still, you gotta have a contract."

Yes, still, you gotta have a contract.

Could you do work without one? Sure. Would I recommend it? No way!

There are lots of great reasons to have a contract. Here's a few:

- It could be required by law. In fundraising in particular, many states have laws requiring a contract (and more).

- It tells everyone you are a professional. Nothing says "I'm real" than a contract. A contract moves your work (in the eyes of your client) from a hobby to a business.

- It removes any confusion that you may be volunteering your services. This is important to clarify in a sector where volunteering is part of the labor force. With a contract up front, there's no confusion at the end of a job when you present your client with a bill.

- It makes you take your work more seriously. "I have a contract to fulfill" maybe what gets your attention to get the job done.

- It can make you look good. If you say in your contract, for example, "only three re-writes," you look great if you "make an exception" and give them four or five.

- It prevents abuse of your time. A contract defines exactly what your job is. Like nonprofits can suffer "mission creep," you can suffer "job creep," if what you are expected to do is not well defined in the contract.

- It draws a definite end date. The best contracts end on a specific date. It's not to say you can't extend them, but a clear date gives you (and your client) the means to rethink your relationship. After all, you may need an "out" if you don't like working with a client.

What's a good contract look like? This is where I'm going to send you to your attorney. S/he probably has some templates for you to review that are specific to consulting. If you are in fundraising (or even if you are not), since contracts files with the state are public documents, you may be able to request a sample from the state agency handling fundraising consultant registration. And while you're at it (again, if you are a fundraiser) make sure that your contract covers the required points as mandated by the state in which your client resides. At least one state (New York) has a form which must be included in all fundraising counsel and solicitor contracts. Most states put their fundraising counsel or fundraising solicitor contract requirement on the same, or linked website, as the website that addresses nonprofit fundraising registration. Oh, and don't forget to register in that state, if it is required.

I try to make the contract development process as easy as possible for me and my clients. This means having an attorney approved template with blank areas for the client information highlighted so I can add the information easily. Since I am in fundraising, I gather all of the state required information in one section so that it is easily seen and approved by the state's reviewer. I put the specifics of the work I intend to do for the client, and the associated pricing, in an appendix (which is referred to in the body of the contract). This becomes an easy reference for my client and me as we move ahead with the project.

There are some sections that you can develop for insertion or removal as the job requires, or if the client request. These include:

- A confidentiality clause. This states that I will not discuss the nature of the project with others, or that maintains the privacy of their clients.

- A publicity clause. This gives me permission to tell others that they are my client, and to use any materials I develop for them as samples for sales purposes. Most client have no objections to this, although some have asked for this clause to be removed.

- A non-hire clause. This states that if I use subcontractors on their job, that they cannot either hire the subcontractor as an employee, or independently contract with that person without my permission or within a certain amount of time after the contract ends.

You or your attorney might think of others.

In some instances, your client will have a "standard contract" of their own, or require you to add specific sections (such as confidentiality). I usually don't object to this, although I suggest you pass it by the eyes of your attorney before you sign. If you are in a state regulated discipline, such as fundraising, make sure that the state mandated provisions are included. This might take some education of your client on your part. I wrote a short "white paper" explaining the state process for my clients, so they know I am being law-abiding, as all their vendors should be, and not needlessly obstructing the process. You could add the state requirements as an appendix, referred to in their main document. (Many clients, even ones that have hired fundraising consultants before, have told me that nobody ever mentioned state contract requirements or approvals before. If you hear this, make clear that you are not needlessly bothering them. It is a law and you are helping them by following the law. The last thing they need is a fine and sanctions from their state attorney general's office.)

Exercise 55

____ Gather any state required contract points from any agency that regulates your discipline.

Exercise 56

____ Contact your attorney about a template contract you can use for your consulting business.

Exercise 57

____ Add any required points to your contract. Re-submit your contract template to your attorney for final approval.

Exercise 58

____ Some states where contract approval is required will do you the courtesy of reviewing your template. Inquire about whether this is possible, and if so, do so.

Your Own Philanthropy

It is worth considering your own attitude toward charitable giving before you start working as a consultant, freelancer or vendor to nonprofits. I am by no means suggesting that you can't work in the field without being charitable (although I think it helps), nor am I saying that you must give to any client. What I am saying, however, is that you could be working in an environment where giving is "normal." Being able to at least understand that point-of-view, if not relating some of your own experiences, can be an asset in developing relationships.

With that in mind, consider working through the exercises in Tracy Gary's "Inspired Philanthropy: Your Step-by-Step Guide to Creating a Giving Plan and Leaving a Legacy" (See the reference section at the end of this book for details.) Gary uses her own experience to bring the reader through a financial planning-like model to help you align your interests with your giving. Many I know are surprised at how much they give to organizations which don't really connect with their values or interest, for all sorts of reasons.

Exercise 59

___ Google "Inspired Philanthropy: Your Step-by-Step Guide to Creating a Giving Plan and Leaving a Legacy." Review the contents to see if it will help you discern your own philanthropic style and relate better to clients. If so, get the book and work on the exercises (after you finish this book, of course!)

Insurance

Do you need insurance? I don't come with the bias of an insurance agent. Still, I'm more risk averse than many, so I think you need it. Some small consultants have it, others don't. One consultant friend who's been in business for more than 10 years mentioned that he never got around to it. Like anything else, you need to weigh the rewards (more short term income) vs. the risks (security from disaster.) You'll definitely need it with some bigger clients who require it, and those smaller ones whose attorney (usually a board member) demands that all vendors and consultants working with them have insurance. Others don't care.

Finding an insurance agent is more than just calling up a local broker. Most insurance agents don't handle business insurance, or at least the kind you might want. Like attorneys and accountants, you need to ask around for a business insurance specialist. The chamber of commerce or local business resource center, like SCORE (https://www.score.org/), are good places to start. Keep in mind as well that these are independent business people like you, so look for networking opportunities.

What kind of insurance are you looking for? Talk to insurance brokers. I've found most recommend two types: Errors and Omissions (commonly known as "E&O") and Liability. E&O protects you from something you did or forgot to do professionally that someone decides that you are responsible for.

Let's say that you're a golf outing event planner and you forgot to tell your client to get hole-in-one insurance. About half way through the event, you hear a roar coming from the 7th hole, where the new car prize for the hole-in-one was sitting. Someone comes running to the clubhouse, all out of breath about the amazing shot that Bob Mulligan made. "It dropped right in! It dropped right in!" he shouts hysterically. After a few moments of celebration, you realize - you forgot to tell your client to get hole-in-one insurance. Who is paying for that car?! Well, it might be you, through your errors and omissions insurance. (By the way, I just made that up for illustration's sake. Always check with your insurance agent to find out exactly what your E&O policy will, and won't cover.)

Liability insurance is for circumstances where someone might slip and fall or otherwise hurt themselves doing something related to your business. As a consultant, you might think that's pretty rare, and I'd agree. Consult your agent about this and the costs.

If you hire someone, your insurance situation, and a lot of the rest of your business life, gets exponentially complicated. Again, ask your agent.

Only you can decide whether what you do is risky enough, what you own is worth preserving, and what revenue you generate is enough to justify the costs. I highly encourage you to seriously inquire, at least so you know for when a client requires it.

How much will it cost? It's hard to say. First, in the United States, insurance is regulated by the states, so it will vary state by state. After that, there is how much dollar amount protection you want, how the company assesses your risk, where you do business (home/an outside office/client sites and where in your state), whether you do business online, and more.

Along with insurance, you may have to get clearances for child protection purposes, and other background checks. In my experience, these are not triggered until in your work with clients, you have contact with certain mission recipients, like children or other vulnerable populations. Again, your client will have policies on this, and you may have to pay for the process. That said, once done, you're cleared for whatever time it's good for, and any client you serve.

Exercise 60

Identify three business insurance agents. Have personal meetings with at least two.

_____

_____

_____

Through your conversations with these agents, decide:

____ If you need insurance.

____ If you need insurance, what kind of insurance do you need.

____ Is this person, and their staff, someone I can feel good calling in an emergency?

Exercise 61

After you leave the insurance office or end the phone conversation:

____ Research whether the company the insurance agent carries is one with a good reputation and financial track record.

Do you need a Vacation?

Do you need a vacation? Yes! I know, you haven't started and we're already talking about vacation. That's because if you don't plan that from the start, you may never get to it. Besides, you need a vacation for all sorts of reasons - physical, and psychological. As motivating as it is to work with nonprofits, and as nice your nonprofit clients can be, getting away will boost your productivity and probably make you happier with your work. At first glance, being able to take vacations "at will" looks like the single major advantage of consulting. After all, your life is totally flexible, right? You set your own hours, select who you work with and work where you want. Just fit it in!

Reality is much different.

While there is no limit to the days you can take, no corporate "use it or lose it" policy and you don't need to worry about how many "PTO" (paid time off) days you took this month, money, time and place loom large in your ability to get a break.

Money.

Money is a major obstacle to a vacation, whether you have a paycheck job or your consulting for nonprofits. It limits what you can do or not, or if you do, where you go and in what style you travel. What's so special about this as a consultant? Rather than a regular paycheck and paid vacation time, as a consultant on vacation, client work doesn't get done. That means there's no paycheck waiting for you when you get home.

You can't prevent this, but you can soften the blow. Start your own "Vacation Club Account." Back in the day, banks offered "Vacation Club Accounts." The idea was to encourage savings year 'round by offering a special short term interest rate. Whether regularly or episodically, the family would add to the account, with the idea that they would withdraw the money right before it was time to take that week at the shore, or the once-in-a-lifetime cross country road trip. Is it time to create your own Vacation Club account?

Time.

Besides losing time on client projects (and thus, income), time impacts a consultant's vacation opportunities in other ways. The kids only have certain times off from school. Your spouse only gets one, two or three weeks a year. Everyone, to some greater or lesser extent, deals with those and more.

Now, layer on top of those your own and your client's business cycles. For example, in direct mail marketing, the prime vacation month of August can be very busy with work because your clients are preparing for fall mailings. On the other hand, December, when your clients are crazy with fundraising, could be light for you because your part of the mailings are done and they're at the printer and post office. You may not get a full grasp of these cycles for a couple of years.

Eating into your vacation time are needy clients, last minute clients, and those whose deadlines fell while you were away but you decided to go anyway. If you take an extended vacation, these issues are magnified. And don't be your own worst enemy, and make your vacation into a mini-business retreat, or, God forbid, take work with you!

Place.

Place is important for reasons you may not expect. If you work at home, a "stay-cation" feels like going to work. If you're in cell phone range, expect calls from clients. A lot of clients don't respect your time off. If you go where you don't have cell service (and yes, those places still exist) you need to be able to resist the temptation to drive down the back woods road to the only hill where you get a bar and a half service to check your voice mail.

So, can you take a vacation? Yes. You need to prepare yourself, and your business and your clients. Here are a few ideas.

- At least a month in advance, let all your active clients know you will be away. Remind them again in two weeks and then the week after that. Try to either get their work done ahead, or schedule deadlines a week past your return. As a last resort, agree to take calls while you are away.

- Set an "away message" on your email. Consider the same for your phone's voice mail.

- Consider having a trusted colleague consultant as a backup. Some consider this risky, because you are giving access to a client by a competitor. You might want to work out a formal "back up agreement" between you and your colleague/competitor before you start.

Exercise 62

Make your vacation plans now! Initiate a discussion with your spouse, family, friend or whoever you usually go with on vacation. Decide the following:

What amount of vacation time will you take (month, week(s), weekends, days?)

_____

Exercise 63

____ Block off those days in your calendar, now!

Exercise 64

Name places you might go.

_____

_____

_____

_____

_____

Exercise 65

Estimate how much money you will need, and when, for a vacation.

_____

_____

_____

_____

_____

Exercise 66

____ Set up a savings plan to meet your vacation plan goals.

4 MARKETING

Self Confidence

Like so much of life, having self-confidence is the key to successfully accomplishing whatever it is you would like to do. Consulting for nonprofits is no different. Does having self confidence in a consulting practice mean you need to be an over-the-top extrovert? No. It means that you need to know you're good, and as much as possible put away the self-doubt about your abilities to do the work (probably the easy part), and get the clients (likely the hardest part).

Putting away self-doubt is hard. Sometimes just being able to talk about what you do is hard. You know all the nuances and details of your specialty, and you're enthusiastic about them. In consulting, selling your services is, in large measure, is less about convincing someone that you have the skills, and more about developing a relationship with the client so she or he feels comfortable with you and your skills. A friend compares it to dating. Sometimes it's just a matter of breaking the ice. If your consulting business requires you to break the ice regularly, you need some self-assurance.

One of the best ways to build self-confidence is to gain formal expertise. You're probably considering nonprofit consulting because you're already an expert in some aspect of nonprofit operations. Building on this by either going deeper into your subject, or widening your expertise, can go a long way to help you show your clients that you have the experience to solve their problem - and assurance that spending their money with you is worth the risk.

Look at this from your client's point-of-view. They're wary of you and anyone who claims they can relive their "pain." Why shouldn't they be? Who are you, anyway? Just someone who says they have a clue. This is why it's essential for you to keep up with trends and technologies, to refute what's nonsense and embrace what's "best practices." It's also why you need to learn how to build trust - of your potential client in you, and you for yourself.

Skill Building

Skill building and education in your field keeps you fresh in the eyes of clients, and more confident of your own abilities. While the basics of any field may remain the same, it's certain that the technology surrounding it and the pace at which it occurs has accelerated. As a consultant, you have no choice but to stay updated on your specialty. The difference is that you are paying for it, not your employer. This is a particular pinch at the start of your consulting career, when cash could be short.

Having opportunities to build your skills usually isn't the problem. Chances are that your discipline's professional organization offers seminars, conferences or credentialing on the latest trends and topics. Here's some of your options:

- Professional associations. It's very likely that your field within the realm of nonprofit management has its own professional association. (Go to ThinkNP.com for a list.) Attending meetings, whether formal training sessions or informal gatherings, is essential. From a business point of view, these are your top potential clients, so you need to be networking with them. From an educational point of view, even the informal gatherings can help you collect important intelligence on the latest happenings in your profession. Make sure that any list of skills includes naming your memberships in professional associations.

- Conferences. Today, conferences are put on by professional associations and private companies. Whichever you attend, conferences serve a number of purposes in our professional life. Yes, they have education components which are very important in our professional development. Besides that, their social gatherings with like-minded, and like suffering, colleagues. You get to network with people that you might not otherwise meet. You collect information on the latest in your field. You have marketing opportunities for your newly considered consulting practice.

- Academic education. Academic education is increasingly available for nonprofit management. This usually comes in the form of master's programs, but there are certainly non-degree certificates available, as well. As you consider academic education, whether it is a degree program or a class here or there, remember that you can pick up skills in your particular chosen profession (like fundraising or nonprofit management), disciplines that are related to your profession (like marketing, or accounting) and other background that might relate to your client's interests (such as environmental, healthcare, social service and more).

- Work experience. It is important to consider the number of months you worked in a particular subspecialty of your chosen profession. For example, were you a fundraiser? How many months did you work in annual fund, major gifts, planned giving, etc. How did each of these contribute to your skills?

- Periodicals. You may not list them for your client's marketing purposes, but receiving on paper or online a number of periodicals specific to your discipline is important to keep up with latest trends. Many of these come with professional associations, but there are also independent publications worth receiving. Since most come both online and in the postal mail, I suggest that you receive both. I'm not suggesting that you hunker down with the latest magazine when you receive it. I use paper copies less for myself, and more to distribute to clients and potential clients. Sometimes there's an article I'd like them to read or simply to build broader awareness of the work I do. Giving away a copy of the physical copy of the periodical is an excellent way to build credibility with the client.

- Internet alerts. Whether you use Google, Bing or another search engine, nearly all will have the capability of generating an "alert" for whatever search phrase you select. I know some colleagues who do this with their client's names and others who want to keep track of specific information of professional interest. Whichever you do, getting a weekly or even daily note via email is a great way of keeping up with what's happening in your chosen specialty.

Now, the real issue is recording everything you do.

It is important that whatever you do for gaining skills in your profession, that you log the activity name, date and summary of your work. Review the list above. As best you can, write down the topic and date of every conference, meeting, seminar or class that you attended, and the periodicals you subscribe to (see below).

I suggest that you use the professional development seminar as your basic unit of education. In other words, if you were to go to a mornings seminar on "how to write grant proposals," you would record that as a seminar attended. If, on the other hand, you were at a conference that had "how to write grant proposals," and "prospect research 101" two of the sessions you attended, list each separately. You don't want to give the impression that a three-day conference was the same as a morning in a meeting room at a local nonprofit. Therefore, treat each conference session as a series of smaller seminars. This will also give you a better view of the breath of education you have in your field.

Once you have culled from memory or past documentation on your work experience and professional development opportunities, it's important to build a skill development plan for yourself, moving forward. Do you see gaps in your knowledge? Is it important to develop skills in an up-and-coming area of your work? You'll find it much better to be systematic and intentional on this rather than grabbing at whatever comes up in the next professional association newsletter.

Exercise 67

List all periodicals you subscribe to, whether on paper or online, including free, regular professional newsletters. Anything missing?

_____

_____

_____

_____

_____

_____

_____

_____

_____

_____

Exercise 68

Begin your list of every professional development conference or session you have attended.

_____

_____

_____

_____

_____

_____

_____

_____

_____

_____

Exercise 69

What gaps do you have in your professional development? For example, are you a direct mail specialist? Have you taken a seminar on writing for email or social media? List where you need to fill in:

_____

_____

_____

_____

_____

_____

_____

Exercise 70

As you look ahead, name three of the most rapidly changing areas of your discipline serving nonprofits. Write them here, and list any seminars you can identify that will address these trends.

_____

_____

_____

_____

_____

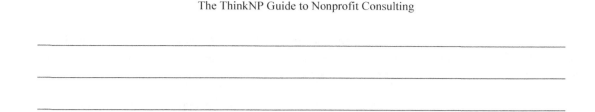

Preparing for Marketing

"Why should I hire you?" is the question that every client asks. Marketing is your answer.

Marketing is not bragging or boastful. Marketing is not sleazy or less-than-honest. Marketing is not extraneous to what you do, whatever it is you do for your nonprofit clients. Marketing is an essential element of your nonprofit consulting practice.

Consider that marketing actually helps your client. It makes them aware of your great products and services so you can help them accomplish their mission. If not for your marketing, how would they know?

Marketing is building favorable awareness of you and your product. "Sales" is just one aspect of marketing. Sales is specifically offering your service in a way that encourages a decision to engage you or not. Marketing is the background actions and information that leads to sales – the networking, branding, pricing and more. Good marketing leads to sales, and after the sale, continued good marketing leads to the next sale.

Contrary to the reputation of the word "marketing," (maybe the concept of "marketing" needs good marketing?) the practice of marketing can be overt and expensive, or subtle and thrifty. You need to find the right balance of marketing tactics that builds your "brand" (think: reputation) and amount and level (quality) of work you are interested in doing.

You have many, many marketing options. You'll find several of them to follow. Regardless of which you choose, you need to be persistent with your favorite two or three. By only picking a small number, you can focus your efforts on methods that match your personality. This will make it much easier to carry them out on a long-term basis. Who knows? Maybe marketing will become fun?!

Before you do anything that even looks like marketing, from your first social media post to uttering the last syllable of your speech, you have some decisions to make.

Are you a commodity?

If you're a commodity, then from your client's point of view, it really doesn't matter who she or he goes to. You are sugar. And when you get down to it, whether it's the store brand or a "premium" brand, sugar is sugar is sugar. To their taste, they're both as sweet.

Don't feel bad. At some level, we're all commodities – in a business sense, that is. You could probably name at least a few people or businesses that do what you do for nonprofits. Most business can. That's just competition, but it doesn't mean you're a commodity. What's the best way you can tell if you're a commodity? You compete on price, alone.

Maybe the best example of an industry that knows it's commoditized is the car insurance business. Just watch their commercials. They know that in the end, insurance is pretty much all of the same. While the average consumer really doesn't know what "good" insurance is, they know what a good price is (or so they think.) Insurance companies know this, too. Competing on price alone is a death-spiral to insolvency.

What's a commodity to do? Maybe give a nod to price, just to assure their customers, but then double down on perception. Today you could buy the lizard, tomorrow go with the flo, and next week enroll at insurance U. When all you have to offer is price, you have to make yourself stand out in the minds of your customers, even if how you stand out is meaningless when it comes to the product, itself.

The good news is that while we know that our nonprofit clients are price sensitive, you don't need to compete solely on price. If you do, you'll end up miserable, and they'll get a poor product from you or the person who undercut you to work for next to nothing. You have an obligation to yourself, and to them, to show them the real difference between you and your competition. You need to prove that price alone isn't a reason to buy.

I'm sure you're relieved to discover that this doesn't mean making up fictional characters or pretend to sell boxes of something that can't be boxed.

You offer a real difference between what you sell and what your competition does. You offer a service in a special way, with results that are as unique as you, and them. Show samples. Show results. Show you understand their mission almost as well as they do.

If you prove your difference, can you charge the stars and the moon for what you offer? Probably not. Can you get a fair price? Yeah, you can.

So before you bury your sorrow in a sack of sweets, remember you are only a commodity if you don't let your clients know you aren't… and they'll be happy to know that there's a real difference.

That brings us to three concepts: Niche, USP and Target Market

Exercise 71

Name how you are not a commodity. List below what is special about you, how you work, your view of your specialty and/or how you deliver your service?

_____

_____

_____

_____

_____

Defining your niche.

Defining your niche can seem terribly limiting, especially in the beginning of a consulting practice. You will face a tension between wanting to do everything for everybody, and narrowly defining your skills and the missions you like to serve. You may never completely resolve this. You know that you can only do so much for so many people. It's hard to put your finger on exactly what it is you do the very best, plus you don't want to say "no" when you could have a client and some income.

Many successful nonprofit consultants, freelancers and vendors are razor-sharp focused on exactly what they do best, and the missions they care most about. Yes, that seems counterintuitive. They could do so much more, and sometimes they do. Yet when they're focused, they see more of what they're focused upon, and can tell others exactly what work they're looking for. Consider this: if you tell someone "I'll do anything," you'll either hear about every bad opportunity that crosses his or her desk, or hear nothing at all. Plus, you'll be so scattered that you will miss opportunities that are perfect for you.

This is not just a nonprofit consulting issue. At one point in my fundraising career, I met a donor whose complete business was accounting for companies who provide linen rental service to hotels for banquets in Manhattan. That was it. I'm sure he was a great accountant and could have plied his trade in any number of industries. But he knew exactly what his strengths were, and dug deep into the business of his clients so he knew exactly how to help them.

This level of specificity is certainly a possibility for your consulting practice. Depending on your area, there might be sufficient numbers of arts nonprofits, or educational institutions, or environmental organizations, or whatever other mission that you feel passionate about. Cross that with your skill specialty, such as fundraising campaigns, or social media marketing or graphic design services, for example and you have defined your niche.

To find your niche, ask yourself:

- Who do I like working with?

- Do I like big picture projects, or a tight focused tasks?

- Do I like "doing" (like grant writing) or "advising" (like campaign management)

- What kind of nonprofit related work have I done?

- What kind of work do I like that I can see doing for a very long time?

- What missions have I worked with?

Know that what you are describing is your ideal. It's not "carved in stone." You can change at any time. You might find, for example, that although you think of yourself as a fundraiser, your clients like your work in marketing. Super. If you like it, go with it and push your consulting into marketing.

Answer the following questions:

Exercise 72

What kind of people do I like working with?

_____

Exercise 73

Do I like the big picture projects or a tight focused tasks?

_____

Exercise 74

Do I like "doing" (like grant writing) or "advising" (like campaign management)

_____

Exercise 75

What kind of nonprofit related work have I done?

_____

Exercise 76

What kind of work do I like that I can see doing for a very long time?

_____

Exercise 77

What missions have I worked with?

_____

Exercise 78

In three sentences or less, describe your niche:

_____

_____

_____

_____

_____

Your USP: Unique Selling Proposition

Once you've defined your niche, it's time to express it in your USP, or Unique Selling Proposition. While your niche is the service you offer to your clients, your USP is how you express that service. Exactly what is it that makes you different from anyone else offering your service, or similar services. What makes you different in:

- Skills

- Interests

- Background

- Geography

- Approach to problem solving

- Network of resources

- Etc.

Can you describe what you do and what's unique about your work in one sentence? Can you describe it to a child? If you hear someone ask you for your "30-second elevator speech," they're asking for your USP.

Here's some examples:

I'm a marketing copywriter for nonprofits and small business in the Philadelphia regional market.

- Type of work: writer.
- Subtype: marketing copy.
- Market: nonprofits and small business.
- Where: Philadelphia region.

I'm a system analyst who helps nonprofits decide the best constituent databases for their mission through a three step, systematic approach to discern their needs.

- Type of work: systems analyst.
- Subtype: constituent databases.
- Market: nonprofits.
- Approach: three step, systematic approach to discern their needs

My photography captures the essence of life's essential moments at weddings and events at a rate that you can afford.

- Type of work: photographer.
- Market: weddings and events.
- Price point: affordable

Your USP doesn't need to capture everything about your work, just enough to make you distinctive from others who do similar work. Besides telling people what you do, a USP builds your self-confidence. Practice saying your USP aloud, and in a way that sounds natural, not contrived. You'll find out what I mean about building your self-confidence.

Exercise 79

Using the above examples as a guideline, create your Unique Selling Proposition

_____

_____

_____

_____

Now that you know what you're doing and what makes you distinctive doing it, who will you do it for? That brings us to your target market.

What's your target market?

Target marketing is a pretty well-known concept. Maybe the simplest way to think about it is "defining who your ideal customers are." By knowing specifically who you want as a customer you'll be able to filter out anyone who clearly isn't, and put your time and energy into learning the likes and dislikes, nuances and habits of those who will be the source of your next job. That helps you "target," or tailor, your marketing to meet their needs.

While it's tempting to say "my target market is nonprofits," it's also far too general to be of any use to you. Let's go a few layers down, starting with the type of nonprofit.

While the most commonly considered nonprofit is what the IRS defines as a "501(c)3," there are nearly 30 kinds of nonprofit organization types, including chambers of commerce, fraternal organizations, cemetery corporations, credit unions and lots more. The (c)3s are notable for providing a tax donation receipt in exchange for a charitable gift. Most of the others can't do that, but otherwise they're typically tax exempt. For the sake of argument, and because it's most likely, let's just say that you're working with a (c)3. (How can you find out your client's nonprofit type? Go to www.Guidestar.org and review their IRS 990 tax form.)

Is there a nonprofit function you focus on? Some functions cross a wide variety of nonprofits. For example, are you a fundraising expert, a finance guru, or a marketing maven? Even within these functions, there are subspecialties. In fundraising, for example, maybe you work specifically with major gifts or direct mail? Other functions are specific to the nonprofit field. For example, it could be that you consult on healthcare delivery systems, social worker training or wetlands conservation techniques.

This leads us to what type of (c)3? Type? Yeah, what's their mission? The nonprofit's "mission" is its purpose, and what makes it different from any other nonprofit, even from ones that do similar work, or in the same general area. For example, how many churches are near you? While they're all the same type, churches, the Last Baptist and the First Methodist might view their missions differently. A good nonprofit mission is focused (and if it's not, maybe that's a consulting opportunity?)

As a consultant, you need not focus on any one of the above. Maybe you can define your target market differently? (Working with female executive directors? Nonprofits in a specific geographic area? Boards who have no staff?)

There's also no reason that you need to stick to a specific target market forever. Some consultants start very narrowly defined (accounting systems for summer camp finances) and expand as they become proficient in their services (nonprofit comprehensive administrative databases.) Others start very broadly (general fundraising), but narrow down to what they do best (major donor prospect research).

However, you define it, your target market is that common thread that makes your marketing much more efficient.

Let's take three steps to define your target market:

Exercise 80

Name three nonprofit types who use the niche that you defined earlier.

_____

_____

_____

Exercise 81

Identify three nonprofit missions you feel strongly about. While you may not work all the time with those kinds of nonprofits, you'll probably work best with those whose missions you love.

_____

_____

_____

Exercise 82

Define your geographic parameters for your ideal client:

_____

_____

_____

It's easy enough to get a list of nonprofits in your area from services such as guidestar.org, or your state's department of state (the typical agency who registers corporations in most states). Organizations that are "grassroots" that have little income or are all volunteer are less likely to use consultants. You will usually find a threshold of revenue that indicates an organization can afford your services, if they are motivated.

Exercise 83

Using the above lists, create a "short list" of sample organizations who are likely to engage consultants among those that use the service you have to offer, and for which you have an affinity.

_____

_____

_____

Exercise 84

Using the above exercises, sum up the top three attributes of your ideal client:

_____

_____

_____

Draw a picture of your ideal client.

Nonprofits, like any organization, are composed of people. From your experience in working inside a nonprofit, or dealing with nonprofits as an employee of another organization, can you describe the decision-maker? What is that person's background? Do they come with a degree in the field, or are they a professional manager? What is this person's typical age? Is it usually a man, or a woman? Are there other demographics that would describe this person?

Exercise 85

Make an illustration of your ideal client's decision-maker.

Yes, make a real drawing. Don't worry about how it looks. You'll be surprised at what putting a" mental image" in front of you will do for your ability to find that person when you are prospecting for clients.

Your ideal client:

You can say "No," really.

For all of the ways that you can find clients, it is important to remember that if you do not feel that you can do a good job for the client, or you don't like something about the client, you can simply say "no, I don't want to work for you." (At least before you sign a contract. After you sign is much more difficult, and could be time to call your attorney.)

This could be the toughest thing you do in consulting. After all, having a client that wants to work with you is almost like having money in the bank. Yet some clients will cost you money. How? Well, you could spend more time with them then you actually bill. More commonly, they can aggravate you in a way that takes away from your work with other clients. Whether for these or other reasons, being able to anticipate problems is an important skill. Therefore, in the beginning of your consulting work, you may end up with clients that years later you would never consider, because by then you will have developed a keen sense of what missions, tasks or client personalities you work best with, or not.

Don't think that you can't fire a client, either. It gets a bit stickier, and if you have a contract, you always want to make sure you fulfill the provisions. Once completed, you can choose not to renew. You can also have a conversation with your contact when you see issues coming up. Chances are, if you feel there are problems, your client does too. Clearing the air goes a long way. You might decide to part ways and come to an agreement on how you get paid (or how much less, or not at all in some circumstances) or a good conversation can get you back on track for successful completion and a long-term engagement. Successful client engagement can be very much like a Rubik's cube. It takes a few turns to get it right.

Exercise 86

Return to your exercise on your target market. Name three (or more) conditions under which you would not accept a client.

_____

_____

_____

Your Brand

What you're starting to build through the exercises above is creating your "brand." A brand is akin to your reputation. Some would say your brand is the perception that others have of you and your business. In independent consulting, you are your brand. It's that simple, especially if you're starting out.

When your client considers engaging you for work, they get you. Maybe you have a clever symbol to represent you. Maybe you have a special way you dress (like bow ties, or scarves)? Maybe you're known for the passion you bring to the work, or your straight forward approach? Those are part of your personal, and now professional, brand. They add to your brand core: you.

A brand is an expectation of service or product as represented by the symbols and actions that surround it. Businesses spend a lot on their brands, and building "brand awareness" is a significant industry. People like to identify with brands. Do you love Apple and advocate for their products when asked? Do you wear a Nike swoop? Did you have a favorite cereal when you grew up? (Or now?) I'll bet you remember its name, the box and the taste. That's all a part of their brand, and so much more - like where it sits on the shelf, and what celebrities or characters pitch it and how much it costs. Brands go beyond the commercial sphere, too. What political brand do you identify with? Do you adhere to a particular faith "brand?" Even countries have a level of brand awareness among those within it, and people from other places.

A brand's objective is to make you "feel" the product or service (or party, or faith or nation) so you're confident in its ability to fulfill your need - and ultimately, "buy" it (whether that's a commercial transaction, a vote, or walking into a house of worship.) If you, as a brand advocate, promote a brand, you strengthen it. If you are inattentive or don't respond well to accidental negative experiences, you diminish your brand. And whether you want it or not, you have a brand, just like you have a reputation.

Right now, consider the external branding basics, like your website, email address, any examples of your work (online or on paper), and testimonials. Yes, how you dress and your manner of speech contributes to your brand, as does your enthusiasm (or not) for your work.

As you develop your brand, ask...

- Am I consistent? (Does my website represent the quality of my work? Do I dress "corporate" but talk in slang?)

- Do I connect my brand with my work? (If you're a graphic designer, do your own sales images look as good if not better than my client's, or does the "cobbler have no shoes?")

- Does my brand connect with my client's needs? (Am I trying to sell high-end product to a downscale market?)

- Do you come across sincere or slick or homey or highbrow? (That's okay if you want to.)

When developing a brand that appeals to nonprofit buyers, consider the attributes of most nonprofits you know (and see the list in the Nonprofit Culture" section.) You want to appeal to their self-image while being authentic to yours.

Exercise 87

Answer the following about your brand (This maybe how people see you/your brand today, or how you want clients to see you/your brand in the not-too-distant future.):

My overall brand image is:

_____

_____

_____

_____

_____

Exercise 88

It is expressed by the following five attributes:

_____

_____

_____

_____

_____

Competitor Analysis: assess your competitive landscape

To me, "competitor analysis" brings up images of stalking your fellow consultants while wearing dark glasses and a trench coat with a fedora pulled down in the front while you take notes in pencil on a small pad, recording their every client.

Luckily, it need not be that complicated, or stealthy. In fact, a lot of people will be glad to talk.

The object of competitor analysis is to see where your niche fits in relationship to others who do the same or similar work. It is not to muscle them out of a job or stealing their clients. Through competitor analysis you should learn about yourself and how you can do business more efficiently. My guess is that you'll even make friends and build collaboration with your competitors, or even get referrals, a nice win/win.

How do you start? Define your competitors.

Answer these questions about *your* work (some of the answers will be found in the exercises above):

Exercise 89

Broadly, what do you do? (such as fundraising, accounting, marketing, etc.)

_____

Exercise 90

Define your skill set more narrowly. What are your top three skills within what you do? (like grant proposal writing, special events organization, auditing, etc.)

_____

_____

_____

Exercise 91

Do you specialize in, or at least prefer, one or more mission types? (health care, social services, environmental, etc.) Name that/those types:

_____

_____

_____

Exercise 92

What geographic area do you cover? (a county, a region, a state...?)

_____

Exercise 93

Look for resources that list people in your area who meet similar criteria to yours. (Professional association directories, chamber of commerce membership list, Google search) How many do you find?

#: _____

Exercise 94

Pick 10 who seem like they are similar to you either in area, age, specialty or another attribute.

_____

_____

_____

_____

_____

_____

_____

_____

_____

_____

Evaluate the presence online via their websites, LinkedIn pages, etc. Start making notes about what work they do, the kinds of clients they serve and what people say about them. On a separate page, gather contact information like their phone number and email address.

Take five and make direct contact. Propose that you meet over coffee or lunch. Say that you are interested in getting to know them and their business better, and to explore ways you can offer each other help. (This is true. You can become valuable resources for each other through this process.)

Exercise 95

Name your five here:

_____

_____

_____

_____

_____

The questions you ask will depend on where you are in the development of your business. If you're just starting out, try these:

- What did you do before you started your business?

- How did you get into your business?

- What did you least expect when you started?

- Any "words of wisdom" for a newbie?

- And the most important question: "what can I do for you?"

- Compare the replies to your questions over several meetings.

- Do you see patterns among the replies?

- Did any opportunities come to light?

- Did your interviewee seem to say that his/her schedule was busy?

What you hear probably won't dissuade you from going into your own consulting practice.

However, you may get a better idea of what you're getting into, and whether you can do well in your chosen niche.

Your basic tools

There are three basic marketing tools that every consultant, freelancer or vendor to nonprofits needs to have. In my opinion, there are no exceptions to this rule. To be considered seriously and professionally, you need all three.

A business card.

For all the attempted electronic substitutes, nothing as yet has replaced this small pocket size reminder of who you are, what you do, and how to contact you. A lot of other marketing material is gone by the wayside. Business cards endure.

So what you need to put on a business card? Start with your name. You need to decide whether you are going to use your formal name, or what people typically call you. We'll talk about it elsewhere in this book, but this begins to get into your "brand."

Once you decide your name, consider the other information that you could add. At minimum, you need a telephone number and an email address. You could add quite a bit more. For example, your physical address. Increasingly, I see business cards without them. With such an emphasis on email and other means of electronic communications, having a physical address on a business card is less relevant than it used to be. Besides, some people like to maintain a level of privacy by not including their physical address. See below for a list of other possible information to include on your card.

I'm a big advocate of using the back of your card. Put something on it like "I met [your name] at: _____ on this date: _____. We talked about:" It's a nice reminder for people to get back to you about whatever topic you discussed.

Also, make your business card reasonably thick. Having a card that has some substance to it is much more impressive than what feels like a small piece of paper in your hand.

One more thing about cards. It may seem like a good idea, particularly at the beginning of your consulting business, to get the least expensive, or even free business cards. If you haven't run into these yet, you'll find at least one company will give you free cards in exchange for their logo on the back. Nothing screams "newbie" than one of these cards. Do yourself a favor and invest a little bit of money into your business cards, even if you have to get fewer to be able to afford the price.

Business Card Possible Lines/Fields:

On Front:

- Name:

- Job Title:

- Company Name:

- Address 1:

- Address 2:

- Email:

- Work Phone:

- Cell Phone:

- Fax:

- Skype:

- Twitter:

- Facebook:

- YouTube Channel:

- Other Social Media:

- QR Code pointing to LinkedIn, Website or YouTube:

- Logo:

On back:

- Slogan or Saying:

- Offer:

- I met [name] at _____,

We spoke about _____

- Skype:

- Twitter:

- Facebook:

- YouTube Channel:

- Other Social Media:

- QR Code pointing to LinkedIn, Website or YouTube:

- Logo:

- Other:

Physical characteristics:

- Curved or Square Corners:

- American or Euro (slightly larger) sized:

- Horizontal or Vertical:

- Base (card stock) Color:

- Text color:

- Other colors:

- Thickness: regular, heavy, extra heavy

- Coating Front: none, matte, gloss

- Coating Back: none, matte, gloss

Creating your business card is easy. The question is how much money you want to spend.

Several online printers offer "drag and drop" self-design based on their templates. I've seen several nice cards made this way – although if you go to enough online sites, you'll start recognizing who used an online template. Many of these same companies also offer in-house design expertise for an additional charge.

Alternatively, you could engage a local designer. This could also be an opportunity to test someone's work for your later partnering for client work. In this case, get a bit more control and personal service, although you may pay more for it. For your final production, you could let your designer use a printer with whom they have a relationship, or get the file in a jpg or another format to upload to an online printer, and order them on your own.

Exercise 96

____ Using the above (and other, if you chose) criteria, create your business card.

Your website

The next business essential for any consulting is a website. First of all, let me say that a Facebook page or a LinkedIn page is no substitute for a website. You need to have a "presence" on the web so that people take you seriously. Secondly, know that you don't need to be a technical expert to make this happen.

It all starts with choosing the right website name. As a good friend of mine would say, "the right name is the name that's available." In other words, you don't have to buy a "premium" name for a premium price. Go to any of the typical website "URL" (Uniform Resource Locator – if you ever wondered) vendors, like GoDaddy.com, 1and1.com, HostGator.com and others.

Play around with the vendor's search tools for either your name or variation of your name, or some description of your specialty. Feel free to be creative. Shorter is better. Avoid hyphenations, 2/to/two (to avoid confusion) and look for a ".com" address. You might find it will take some time to find exactly what you like. That said, I'm always surprised at what is available, as well as what's taken.

Exercise 97

____ Go to a popular web domain company (GoDaddy, HostGator, 1and1, etc.) and use their domain name finder to find a domain name to your liking.

Exercise 98

____ Discuss your choices with a friend or close adviser.

Exercise 99

____ Buy the name.

Once you have your website address, consider using the tool that comes with the company that sold it to you to build a website. These have become very easy to use. Most are "drag-and-drop" so you don't need a lot of (or really, any) technical expertise. You don't even need to have more than a single web page. Make sure you have links to whatever social media you are keeping up with, such as LinkedIn and Facebook. Once you generate some business, consider making one of your first investments an upgraded website, built by a professional.

Note: Some of you are screaming "Use a real program like WordPress to design your website!" At one level I agree. WordPress is great (as are other similar, more modern web site building programs). Most are flexible programs with many, many design and function features. However, I have seen people with very little (or no) web site creation expertise build a solid, basic website from a "drag and drop" domain name company website creation application. For what is possible, my recommendation is based on time. I would rather see you, as a nonprofit consultant without a website, get online quickly, albeit not 100% perfectly, than to get absorbed into hours of what maybe frustrating work. Chances are that if/when you engage a professional to design a site, even if you used what they use, it will change drastically and all of your time will be wasted. At that point, I would rather you spend time learning how to maintain your new, professionally created site, than building one now that won't last long.

Important: Own your own website name. If you go with a design firm (or anyone else) to develop your website, make sure you own your website name, not them. Too many consultants and others in business let their designers buy the name because the designer may have a company from which they buy all their client's names. That's a legitimate reason to let your designer handle the purchasing process (although probably for a fee, to you). The problem is that some (unscrupulous, in my opinion) designers end up owning the name, and not their clients. This becomes a major issue when you change designers or the designer goes out of business. You may suddenly lose your entire online identity.

Exercise 100

____ Create a one-page website using the tool provided by the domain name host.
or
____ Identify and contact web designers in your area to price out a more fully developed web presence.

Your email address.

Now that you have a URL and have started a website, create an email address based on that URL. A Gmail, AOL, Hotmail or other general email service is not nearly as professional looking as your own custom email. Again, this does not take a tremendous amount of technical expertise. You simply use the dashboard that comes with the URL you bought to forward the email address you create to your primary email, like your Gmail account. In Gmail, you can filter your emails so that your consulting emails go to a particular place in your box.

Exercise 101

____ If you buy the domain name, create an email address according to the instruction provided by your web domain company (GoDaddy, HostGator, 1and1, etc).

So, are you an expert? Can you prove it?

Even if you have lots of experience and attended dozens of seminars, a client isn't quite sure you're an "expert."

Put yourself in their shoes. If you were your client, or more importantly, a prospective client, how could you tell if you were an expert in your discipline? You (or they) usually can't. They're forced to take your word for it, and if they in any way don't trust you, or themselves, they won't risk giving you their hard earned grant or donor's money to find out.

How do you prove your expertise to your potential nonprofit clients? Here's four ways:

- Your portfolio.
- Success stories.
- References and testimonials.
- Statistics.

Your Portfolio

When trying to prove your expertise, nothing speaks louder than real examples.

For many consultants, it's easy to show a number of samples of your work. Having this readily available in a specific computer file, or better yet, on an online portfolio page attached to your website (not necessarily available to the public, but the URL you can provide when you think it's appropriate for client) can go a long way in proving you can do the job.

Exercise 102

Start gathering your portfolio material. Can you find a dozen examples of your work? Name them here, and list where to find them.

Piece: Where Found:

_____

_____

_____

_____

_____

_____

_____

_____

_____

_____

_____

_____

Gather your Success Stories

People learn by stories. A good story is one of the most powerful human learning methods. Just think about the retention you have after a great movie, verses what you can remember from a chart of donor names you reviewed the other day.

Do you have a story bank? What's that? The story bank is a set of small, one page or less descriptions of your accomplishments. When I recommend a story bank to a nonprofit, it's about gathering success stories about how they served their mission recipients. They can be unique and unusual ways that their mission was express, or solid standard approaches to helping their client, or both.

I want you to do the same. What can you point to as your proudest moments in your professional career thus far? What was the problem? What are the obstacles? How did you overcome those obstacles? What was the result? It's even better when you can show that the client either earned money, or saved money as a result of your engagement.

Gathering these stories is a great way of not only building your self-confidence in your own work, but more importantly to have information that you can address in print, or in person with a potential client. Of course, be sensitive to detailed personal or organizational information. Consider "changing the names to protect the innocent" (for all of you who watched "Dragnet" reruns) so that you don't upset anyone, get into legal issues, or violate confidentiality agreements. If in doubt, review your contract with the client for permissions and/or consult your attorney.

Exercise 103

Think back. What were your top five professional accomplishments in the discipline you are consulting? Name the titles of five and write a one-page story on each.

_____

_____

_____

_____

_____

Exercise 104

Check off after each story is complete:

1._____   2. _____   3._____   4. _____   5._____

How do you use these stories? In voice (telling the story), on website pages, as stand-alone pdf or paper samples, videos, podcasts and lots of other ways.

Testimonials and References

Not only should you say good things about what you did in the form of stories, but others should say good things, too. These come in two forms: testimonials and references. They're very similar in that you have people who have experienced the results of your work make positive statements about you – like the quality of your work, the timeliness, how easy you were to work with, etc.

However, testimonials and references differ in their form and use.

I define "testimonials" as positive shorter statements made about your work, preferably from clients. By this definition, testimonials range from a paragraph to one line or a few words. Most potential clients do not read longer testimonials unless they are very compelling. My recommendation is that you keep your testimonials as short as possible. Testimonials can be used in "sell sheets" (see below), web sites, brochures and other places where a one or two-line statement from someone who can emphasize a point or endorse a particular aspect of your work. A typical testimonial might be "Bob got his project done on time and under budget, saving us thousands!" Or, "I found Josie easy to work with and effective with our volunteers."

References come in two basic forms: phone/verbal and written. Sometimes your prospect just wants names and contact information of people who can talk about your work. Just like with a job search, have references lined up ahead of time, having given permission to provide their names and welcome a call.

Other times they're looking for letters, typically one page, that may include the name and description of a particular project, describe how you were to work with, and inform the reader of any results. Your reference may also offer him or herself as a contact if the reader had further questions. If asked for at all, a prospective client will ask for a reference (or several) during or right before the completion of a contracting process.

While you can get a testimonial or reference from just about anyone who knows your work, this is where titles mean a lot. Getting a good word from the President of New Britain State University is much more meaningful to the reader than from the Assistant Director of Purchasing at NBSU, even though most of your work was with the Assistant Director. Also, the best testimonials are from people who will give their real and complete names. "Harry W. from New Britain, PA" is not nearly as powerful as "Harold T. Windsor, Ph.D., President, NBSU." Make it even more powerful with the person's real photo. I do not suggest you use testimonials that you made up or that you attribute to fake people. If you're starting out and you don't have any clients who can write testimonials about your work, solicit them from past co-workers or bosses. Replace them when you're more established.

When asking, like anything else, you need to put yourself in your reference's shoes. First of all, ask yourself "what's in it for them?" You'd be surprised. Consider reciprocating. As long as you feel good about the other person's work, you might write her or him a LinkedIn endorsement, a recommendation letter for a job in the future, or say a good word to his or her boss.

However, I would stop short of payments for references or testimonials, and I even think material favors or free services start getting into questionable ethical issues. If that comes up, simply say "that's not what I had in mind," and move on.

More likely, your reference will wince at the burden of writing something for you. It's not because they don't like you or your work, it's because to many, nothing is scarier than a blank page. Plus, they have enough to do already! Besides, your reference might think she or he knows what you want, but when you see it, it's totally off track.

Therefore, whether written or verbal, a line or a page, don't leave what someone says about you, to chance: write the reference or testimonial for them. Even better: provide several options. Make it clear (and sincerely mean it) that what you provided is simply a suggestion out of courtesy and respect for their time, and that he or she may change, adjust, or throw away what you offered. At minimum, it gives your reference some parameters. At best, they'll pick one or two of your samples and get them back to you much more quickly than you expected. Because you offer samples as a guideline, and as a time-savings tool for them, and because they can make any changes they want, I do not see this as an ethical issue.

I have to tell you, that as a sales tool, the psychology of testimonials and references fascinates me. To start, nobody knowingly solicits a testimonial or reference from someone they think will give them a bad evaluation. Everyone knows that: you, your client and the people giving the testimonial or reference. Yet even with this knowledge, a third-party statement is among the most influential pieces of your marketing material. The perception is that your work must be good if someone who is not you, or under any other influence than to like your work, says it is good.

Exercise 105

Name five people, with job titles and contact information, who you could approach for testimonials, reference letters or reference phone calls:

_____

_____

_____

_____

_____

Exercise 106

Write five testimonial lines you could offer the above persons:

_____

_____

_____

_____

_____

Exercise 107

____ On a separate page, write a recommendation letter that you could provide one of the people on your list above. Include information on a specific project, your accomplishments on that project, and information on how you were to work with.

Statistics

While I'm the first one to say that "stories beat stats," you need to have the statistics to back up your stories. Can you show that your work increased revenue to your former client? The problem with this approach is that you need to remember to ask for the numbers from your clients, preferably before they stopped becoming your clients. It's easy to do great work for a client. In the rush to get the next task done, it's not often easy for the client to get you the numbers that prove your great work. Be persistent.

Exercise 108

- Gather whatever statistics you have on your work that shows for a past employer or client that you:

    o Increased income

    o Increased clients/participants/donors/members

o Saved money

o Reduced time

_____

_____

_____

_____

_____

_____

_____

_____

Of course, having all of these lined up before you encounter your next potential client is much easier than having to rush around to get them when they're looking for a proposal in less than a week. Building these and other ways to prove your client that you are the best professional they can hire for their mission might not get you every job, but it will make getting any job much less stressful.

All of this isn't just for your clients, however. It's for you. It builds your self-confidence.

Create a Sell Sheet, because a resume won't do.

The other day, at my nonprofit consultant's networking group, I met someone interested in breaking into grant proposal writing. He had a strong academic background, a mature attitude, a passion for a couple of kinds of nonprofit missions, and seemed to be a pretty nice guy. Best of all? He followed up on our meeting with a "good to meet you" email. So far, so good.

It's what he attached to that email that gave me pause. His resume.

I'll hold back commenting on the resume itself. It wasn't bad. It just needed some tweaking.

Regardless, I shouldn't have received a resume. What he needed to send me was a "sell sheet."
You see, a resume, by its very nature, is about you. Not only that, it tells the recipient that you're looking for a "paycheck job," not a consulting engagement.

Instead, a sell sheet makes clear that you are looking to provide your services on a temporary basis – a consulting or freelance basis. And while a sell sheet is about you, it's only about you as a means of telling your potential client how you can help them. Besides, the structure is different. Visually it doesn't say "job hunter." It says "consultant."

What's a sell sheet look like?

At the top: your name, your business' name (if you have one), and if you have a logo and/or a tagline, then that too.

You can choose to put your contact info next, or you can put that at the bottom. Where ever it goes, all you need is a name, phone number, email and a LinkedIn address (and if you have your own website – then add that, too.)

Consider adding your picture. You can decide where it looks best (and if you're tricky enough with your word processor to insert the picture in place and do a text wrap around it.)

Below that, a very brief (three lines at most) paragraph characterizing your background. "Fundraising professional with 15 years' experience in direct mail, management and databases at the following organizations…."

Next, bullet point columns on the skills and services you bring to your clients. Maybe another on the missions you want to serve.

If you have past clients to highlight – here's a place. Even better? One line testimonials.

That's it. Oh, and make it a pdf so everyone can open it.

If they want a resume, they'll ask. Start with a Sell Sheet to provide a brief "snapshot" of you so your client knows what you offer, and will want to ask for even more information or a meeting.

So, remember… resume for jobs, sell sheet for consulting.

Exercise 109

____ Develop a one-page "Sell Sheet" based on the above.

Creating a Bio

If you're going to do any kind of writing or presenting, or anything where someone will introduce you to an audience or want to refer to your background, you're going to need a bio. Actually, you'll need more than one bio, and you'll need to update it regularly.

The purpose of the bio is to provide your audience with one or more compelling reasons to pay attention to what you have to say. This could be based on your years of experience, type(s) of experience(s), past clients or employers, type of business specialty, personal background or anything else that makes you stand out from others. You need not embellish beyond reality in your bio. You are a competent professional worth paying attention to for your expertise.

For all bios, the key to writing is not in the written word at all, it's in the spoken word. Even though your bio may end up on a book jacket or in a conference program website, write it with the idea that someone will be standing at the front of an auditorium (which is certainly possible) reading your bio to the audience. That means paying attention to cadence, keeping your sentences tight, and only use as much jargon as absolutely necessary.

Unless you're really good at it, leave humor or novel openings or endings out of your bio. Yes, there is definitely value in entertaining. There's also a chance of your target audience misunderstanding your humor or novelty, or worse.

All bios will be in paragraph form. In the long format you could afford to have brief bulleted lists.

Consider starting your bio with your name. "Matt Hugg is…" Who you are and why they should care is really what the audience is looking for.

Leave personal stories and information out unless they absolutely relate to your topic. I appreciate the compulsion to humanize yourself, but really, what do you and your audience get out of your saying you own three cats, two dogs, a parrot and an iguana unless you are head of an animal shelter?

Name past employers that might get recognition. You're not applying for a job. Your bio is too short to be a "full disclosure" document – even in a full page format. Name the past employers your audience would recognize, and/or the positions they would respect.

Focus on accomplishments that are related to the work you now do or the presentation you are giving. "Raised $10.8 million in support of bird migration research" would be great for a gathering or ornithologists.

Unless it is important for your audience to know your degree(s) or what you studied, your education should go at the end. If you have a degree with an honorific, like "doctor," then referring to yourself as "Dr. [name]" will imply that you have the education. In the shorter formats, it may be all you need or can fit. Otherwise, if pressed for space and it adds to your prestige, name the highest degrees first, and consider leaving out the lower ones. Don't put anything in lower than a college degree, unless it is important to the program.

The Long Bio: a "long" bio is no more than one page. It's a summary of your career, somewhat akin to a resume. You might think since it's long, the format is flexible. Not really. You just get more information. Think of the Long Bio as the one on which the shorter forms will be based.

Half Page Bio: Yes, shorter. Maybe 100 to 150 words?

Brief Bio: Some will want a bio as short as 25 words. It's a challenge. Focus on exactly what you are doing now and how it relates to the use of the bio.

Exercise 110

____ Develop Long Bio

Exercise 111

____ Develop a Half Page Bio

Exercise 112

____ Develop a 25-word bio

A special note: Giving it away.

In the upcoming section on specific methods of marketing, you might ask yourself, "if I do that, won't I be giving away all my secrets? Why would they hire me instead of doing it themselves?" In particular, this will come up in Speaking, Teaching, Webinars, Writing and maybe some others.

You are exactly right to be concerned... You will be giving away some of your "secrets." It's how you will prove to your audience (who are potential clients, you hope) that you know what you are doing.

You are perfectly wrong to be concerned... For better or worse, most people who go to a seminar (which is your most likely venue to present information) are not likely to implement all that they hear or see. Once anyone returns to their office, they have dozens of other urgent matters to attend to. The chances of them implementing all that you said is very low. At best, they'll do a few things that really stick.

It is also true that those who are good enough to grab your information and run with it are not likely to be your clients anyway. As the saying goes, "your first competition is your potential client." Bless them and let them go. They might even rave about you to their friends about how your seminar was great.

It turns out that most attendees or readers will see how great you are at what you do (thus, increasing your brand recognition among who they tell), and among them, you'll prove your expertise to those who say to themselves "that's complicated/time consuming/difficult, I need to hire him/her to do that for me!"

I confess that I have learned to be a bit more circumspect with the information I provide in one-to-one potential client meetings. This is where I feel you can give away too much while trying to prove your worth. Eventually you'll learn the balance, and don't feel bad if you make mistakes along the way. We all do.

Where do first clients come from?

Your first clients could be a trade-off between experience and money. You need experience, so you give great consulting at a bargain price. Many consultants, from a wide variety of disciplines that do not deal with nonprofits specifically take this approach. They will work with a nonprofit to develop a portfolio on a "pro bono" basis. The advantage that you have as someone who will work with nonprofits long after any volunteer or low-cost assignment ends, is that you have work product directly relevant to future clients and a potential referral base from the clients you do low-cost or volunteer work for.

A number of years ago I was the subject of one of these situations. A person who was building a public relations business asked if she could do free work on my behalf for a particular project. It struck me as odd at first, but I soon understood where she was coming from and was glad and grateful to participate. She did an excellent job and it was helpful in moving that aspect of my business ahead. I certainly recommended her to others, including nonprofits I work with.

Speaking with fellow consultants, I've found that people took a variety of approaches to get their first client. Some started with their last employer on a freelance basis. Of course, this is very dependent upon how you left that position. If favorably, and the organization needs episodic help to handle work that either you had done in the past or new projects that arise, this could be an excellent opportunity. You certainly know the organization well enough that you don't have to be trained on its background or culture. If and when you do this, you want to be sure that you meet the criteria for a contractor as stated by the Internal Revenue Service. While the person who engages you to do the work, your former boss, may not be too concerned about it, the HR office and finance function of the organization will want to make sure that everything is lined up so that it is clear that you are a contractor, not a rehired employee.

Similarly, you could look to other past employers for work. Again, you come with some background that could be helpful.

Don't overlook friends and family. They may be engaged in work with nonprofits that could use your help. Of course, don't say "can you get me a job with the nonprofit you volunteer for?" Most people would find that off-putting, and unless you really know that it's possible, you may do more harm than good in your relationship. Rather, simply ask the person for a contact in the organization and whether you can use your friend's name as a door opener. Even better is if your friend can make an introductory call or email. After that, make the appointment and talk about the organization's needs and how you might provide a solution to them. Remember, just like a nonprofit is focused on who they serve through their mission, your mission is to serve your clients. So this meeting is not about you, it is about the potential client and how you can help.

Exercise 113

Make a list of any past employers and contact names who could be among your first clients.

Organization Name   Contact Name

_____

_____

_____

_____

_____

_____

_____

_____

Exercise 114

Make a list of family and friends who volunteer with nonprofit organizations.

_____

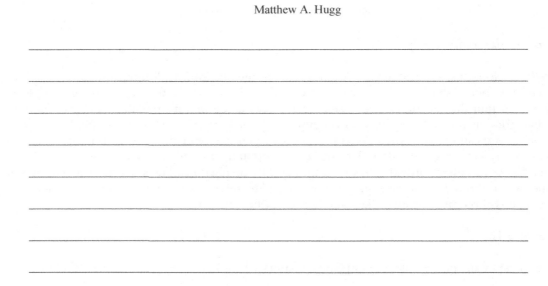

How do you get client 2, 3, 4…?

Sales is different from marketing. They are very closely related to each other. Marketing builds a broader awareness of your product or service. Sales is when the transaction occurs.

For all of the marketing you do, your specific, intentional contact (otherwise known as a "sales call") might be all your prospective clients need that final nudge for a sale to occur. Regardless of whether you are doing mailings by paper or computer, advertising online or in a magazine, using social media or going to professional associations, it is essential that somebody pick up the telephone, sit down in front of a keyboard, or see you at their office or yours for the final transaction to occur. It is essential not to hide behind your marketing message and expected to do a job that it was not meant to do: personally communicating with somebody.

This means that you need to build a real relationship with a "decision-maker." (As they are called in sales.) The decision-maker is exactly how it sounds. He or she is somebody who has the final say about whether a contract is signed so that you can move ahead with your project and get paid.

I'm not suggesting that the marketing work you do is for naught. Good marketing will influence current and future decision-makers on whether you are the person to engage for their project or service. You need to do this to take advantage of your marketing so that when you encounter the decision-maker, as my mother would say, "your reputation precedes you." If you've done the job right, you will have a very positive reputation before you even get into the door.

While there are hundreds of books on sales and sales techniques, it all comes down to this: ask. If you don't ask, nobody will give. (Sounds a lot like a charitable gift, right?) Like charitable giving, asking is best done in person. Telephone is a poor substitute, and paper or electronic mail is worse yet.

Also like charitable giving, it is ideal that you would get a telephone call from a client who is already decided to engage you, rather than you having to pursue them for a conversation about their need. Either way, remember that you offer a good and valuable service. It's likely that they need your service at some point sooner than later. Your job is not to convince them to use your services if they don't need them. That would do neither of you any good. Your job is to make them aware of how your services can help them meet their mission in a way that is of either higher quality, less expense, or better timed than anyone else like you can do - especially themselves. (Remember, your biggest competition is not somebody who does something like what you do, but the client his or herself. Whether do-it-yourself is advised or not, it's usually perceived as less expensive than anything you can offer.)

All this means, is that when it comes to sales, you need to be in front of people. To do that, I've met consultants who swear that you need to "cold call" to generate any measure of sales. (For an excellent cold call book, see Stephen Schiffman's "Cold Calling Techniques (That Really Work!)." I know others who depend on networking and very targeted ways as a follow-up to their marketing. Many times this includes getting to know people who are outside your target field who have contacts inside it. For example, as a graphic designer it might be good for you to get to know writers who work for nonprofits. Many times one "trade," like a plumber, is asked to refer people from allied trades, like carpenters and electricians. You want to be the one that your fellow "trades" refer.

I also highly encourage you to be systematic in your sales. Invest in a customer relationship management program (CRM) to track your interactions and next steps. Ask yourself "how many contacts can I make today?" Your CRM should be able to help you decide. If you're going to be in a certain part of your region, or traveling outside your region, ask yourself "who is in that area that I should visit?" Just check your CRM.

This is predicated upon your having names in that CRM. As mentioned elsewhere in this guide, one of your early tasks should be to write down everybody you know personally and professionally. That's the core of your database. As you go to professional events and see people in other venues, add those to your CRM. You'll be surprised at how quickly these names accumulate.

Exercise 115

____ Begin to build a database. Open a spreadsheet (to start) into which these names will go. Into that spreadsheet, add:

____ All your names in Gmail Contacts, Outlook or other program where you keep contact names.

____ Any business cards you've collected.

___ Any "Rolodex" card file you have with current contacts.

___ Names from your social media connections.

Social Media

Today, it seems like the first marketing method anyone thinks of is social media. Time and again I hear of new consultants planning to rely on their social media connections to rain business down on them. After all, it's cheaper than paper mail, easy to use and you have all of those friends, right?

Yes, but is it effective? Maybe.

Social media is great for chatting among friends about the latest celebrity or family gossip, or following your favorite hobby group. When it comes to generating business, it's a great adjunct. It's rarely an effective stand-alone strategy. You need to combine it with other marketing methods to be most effective.

With the ever constant changing of the social media environment, it would not be a great idea for me to get deep into the details of how one social media platform works versus another. There are many good resources for you to get that information. Rather, let's look at how social media fits into your overall nonprofit consulting marketing plan.

The basics are just this simple: be where your clients are. You don't need to put something out on every platform. When you see an email or social media feed cross your screen about the latest on character counts in Twitter, or whether Facebook will accept one kind of advertisement or another, you don't need to worry about it unless either Facebook or Twitter is how you communicate with clients.

Therefore, find out who among your clients or prospective clients uses which social media channel. Remember, that when I say "use," I mean professionally. Unless you feel it is important to connect with your clients on their off hours, or if you know that throughout the day someone is using their personal social media account while they're at work, you are best off to grab their attention when they are in a "work mode." In fact, seeing an advertisement or an engagement on a platform that they consider "personal" may do you more harm than good.

As of this writing, in my opinion, there are really four social media platforms for you to consider.

- LinkedIn. LinkedIn is probably the most work oriented social media platform popular in the United States, today. Whether or not you use it as a means of communication for your clients, it is important to have a robust LinkedIn profile as a passive advertising means for your consulting practice. If you choose to get deeper into LinkedIn, consider the paid service for more access to information. Remember, you can post information, seek endorsements, seek testimonials, look for clients and potential clients and more. You might even use LinkedIn as a prospecting tool.

- Facebook. Many of your clients may communicate to their clients through Facebook. That does not mean, however, that they want to hear from you this way. It wouldn't hurt to have a Facebook page and update it on a regular basis. Solicit "likes" as you expand your network of contacts. At some point you'll discover whether your efforts are bearing fruit or if you should simply make your Facebook page more static. My experience is that many clients see Facebook as their personal domain, and not for business. Test that out among your clients with personal conversations.

- Meetup. Meetup is an interesting hybrid of the personal, in face connection fueled by a social media platform. You might find that using the Meetup program will enable you to network more effectively for starting your own networking group. It's worth experimenting to see if you get some traction with this.

- Twitter. I have a colleague who uses Twitter quite effectively. She's built a nice audience, and has made a good habit of tweeting on many important items as she moves throughout her day. She's using it as an excellent platform to inform her constituents about the latest in her discipline and other nonprofit oriented topics that she encounters. No doubt, her Twitter feed has become a valuable resource for her clients.

Exercise 116

____ Update (or create, if you do not have one) your LinkedIn profile. For guidance, consider "LinkedIn & Social Selling for Business Development" by Brynne Tillman.

Exercise 117

____ As you network (personally contact potential clients) ask them about what social networks they engage in for business purposes. After talking to at least 10 contact, review the results of your "survey" and decide which channel on which to build your presence.

Special events

Only occasionally have I seen consultants, freelancers or vendors to nonprofits engage in special events as a marketing tool. As I reflect on this, the infrequency of special events as a marketing tool among nonprofit consultants seems rather odd since special events are a major way that client nonprofit organizations raise money and build their reputations. Maybe it's time to learn from the nonprofits on this one?

Of course, the obstacles are just as big, if not bigger for you than they are for the nonprofit. To start, special events can be expensive. Remember, this time it's only you, not a staff of volunteers (or you could hire a special event consultant – maybe one who does nonprofit events, too?). It's very helpful to have a theme, such as your launching your consultancy, or an anniversary of some sort. And then you need the attendees. Like I said to my staff, years gone by, if nobody shows up to an event, it doesn't count. Who can you invite? Clients and potential clients, colleagues in allied but not competing consultancies (for example, if you are a writer, you might invite one or two designers or printers) and others in your network who can speak well of you after the gathering. Having a short program is nice, anywhere from an announcement about something for your business (like telling everybody that this is your kickoff party and to think of you when they need services such as yours) or leading a discussion on some topic of interest to the community or your clients (like the need to develop young nonprofit leadership to replace retiring baby boomers.) Whatever the topic or activity, make it something that everybody can get behind.

An alternative to independently hosting an event is to offer to host a mixer, or sponsor an event for a local nonprofit professional association. It need not be an extravagant affair. A simple after work garden party for one of your association's committees as a "thank you" might be a good place to start. The advantage of working through local professional association is the list of potential attendees. The association will work to get people to show up, so that you can focus on the mechanics of the activity.

Another spin on the special events theme is to host an event for the benefit of a particular client or your favorite nonprofit organization. This may or may not preclude you from inviting people who are with other nonprofits and potential clients. Your other consultant, freelancer or vendor connections might not see it as a business opportunity either. Like an association, hosting an event on behalf of a nonprofit organization might encourage their assistance in its development. (Although some nonprofits are keen on your developing and hosting an event as a fundraiser without their involvement except to receive the donations generated.) Regardless, hosting an event and the associated publicity either broadly or through smaller networks could benefit your consulting.

Exercise 118

Develop a special event theme for your consulting practice (kickoff, anniversary, fundraiser, other?):

_____

Exercise 119

_____ On a separate sheet, make a list of who you would invite to a special event.

Exercise 120

_____ Outline/Develop a short "program" for your event. It maybe a few words thanking everyone for attending, or a more developed presentation on a topic of interest.

Exercise 121

_____ Do you feel bold? Set a date and get planning!

Attending events

On the other side of hosting an event, is attending events. In the biggest communities you can develop a robust social calendar attending networking events on a regular basis. Even in the smallest towns you'll have "go to" activities that you, as the community leader you are becoming, you'll want to attend. (Whether you defined your "community" geographically, professionally, or socially.)

First on your list should be any opportunities to interact with your nonprofit client base. Professional associations are top on this list, as are some nonprofit targeted Chamber of Commerce activities. You may even find organizations focused around a mission purpose (like hospitals, for example) rather than a professional skill purpose (like accountants to nonprofit organizations.) where ever you go, don't be afraid to tell "anyone and everyone" that you're a consultant. Describe your niche and your target market, too.

Target the events to attend. Create a list of local and national professional and community networking organizations where you live or that you are eligible to join (check ThinkNP.com's list for a starter). Include the following information:

- What is the cost of membership?

- Who is the target audience?

- What activities does this organization offer?

- How can interaction with the target audience advance your career goals?

- Who do you contact to join?

- Do you need sponsorship to join?

- Who do you know that already belongs to this organization?

- Can I attend an event without joining a group, and for how much?

- Should I join the organization sponsoring the event? What's the cost?

Determine what groups are best for you to visit regularly based on your mission and vision statements. Almost all states have state-wide nonprofit associations, and the associations have their own association (who would have thought?): The National Council of Nonprofit Associations (www.ncna.org). These groups sponsor events and activities that are often well worth attending for networking purposes. Some regions have "nonprofit centers," usually hosted by a local university, that serve as an educational resource and networking hub. Check out your local chamber. Many host programs focused on their local nonprofit community. Now could be the time to look into the local Toastmasters, Kiwanis Club, Rotary, Elks, Freemasons, book club or sports association (such as a bicycle club or softball league.) This adds an element of personal fun, education or fellowship to your networking routine, making it much easier to schedule.

How do you select where to go? Go for variety. Make sure you pick at least one nonprofit related organization, but then start looking at your community resources. Be systematic about working the list, knowing that some groups won't be a good "fit." Don't forget that many organizations have a number of nearby chapters. One group may seem like a bunch of cold aliens, and the other welcoming and supportive.

If you've never done well at group networking, or if you need a refresher, get a copy of Susan RoAne's "How to Work a Room, 25th Anniversary Edition: The Ultimate Guide to Making Lasting Connections--In Person and Online."

Exercise 122

Create a list of local and national professional and community networking organizations where you live or that you are eligible to join. Include the following information:

- What is the cost of membership?

- Who is the target audience?

- What activities does this organization offer?

- How can interaction with the target audience advance your career goals?

- Who do you contact to join?

- Do you need sponsorship to join?

- Who do you know that already belongs to this organization?

- Can I attend an event without joining, and for how much?

Put your names here (rest of information on can go on a separate document):

_____

_____

_____

_____

_____

Speaking

Speaking is another excellent way of building your reputation as an expert in the nonprofit consulting. It's also one of the most difficult. As I'm sure you've read and maybe even feel yourself, public speaking is a greater fear that even death for many, many people (at least according to Jerry Seinfeld: http://www.forbes.com/sites/jerryweissman/2014/06/17/another-humorous-view-on-the-fear-of-public-speaking/).

Still, it may be well worth your time to master the art. Maybe because of the above-mentioned fear, professional associations have a very difficult time filling speaking slots for conferences. So if you can get good at it, you'll be in demand.

There are plenty of references (see book sources at end of chapter) on how to be a better public speaker, developing PowerPoint presentations and the like. If you want a more intensive experience, consider joining an organization like Toastmasters, or attend a chapter meeting of the National Speakers Association. These are places where the best gather to hone their skills. They're also very welcoming to "newbies."

Over the last several years I have found that speaking to nonprofit professional associations is different than speaking to associations of business persons. For example:

- While both kinds of groups want real information, and not 60 minutes of advertising, associations of nonprofits tend to be more cautious about you, a person in business. Some will even require that you partner with a nonprofit professional in giving your presentation.

- I've never been involved in a speaking engagement at a nonprofit association where, if you have a book to sell, they allow or encourage "back of room" book sales after your talk.

- Rarely do nonprofit associations pay speaker fees. At best, you'll get mileage. The one exception is for keynote speakers.

It's best to be prepared with fresh content year after year. For several years I was asked back to speak at a particular conference. I always use that opportunity to develop my "stock presentation" that I would offer to other groups throughout the year. However, being asked to speak on an ongoing basis is rare. Many organizations will not allow anybody to speak before a hiatus of at least one, and sometimes several years.

Know also that it is likely you will be asked to "apply" for your speaking place. Some of these forms look like job applications. Don't let this process intimidate you. Many times this is a formality. It really depends on the demand for speaking slots. You may also find that while you are turned down for the organization's conference, they will pick you up for one of the several independent programs the organization offers throughout the year. For some organizations, their non-conference seminars are a "farm system" for their regular major conference.

One more hint: always ask about the possibility of videotaping your talk. It's good for website use and other promotional opportunities.

Exercise 123

List three possible topics in your area of expertise for a prepared talk of 30 to 45 minutes. Consider both "traditional favorites" that discuss the basics, and "cutting edge" that address some aspect of some aspect of your discipline's work that is trendy (for trend ideas, search your discipline's trade journals.)

_____

_____

_____

Akin to speaking is teaching.

The major difference between the speaking and teaching is the level of commitment, on both your part and your audience's. Nonprofit management academic programs are much more popular today than ever before. They come in the form of certificates and academic degrees from higher education institutions to professional association "diplomas" on many of the same topics. Unlike seminars or conferences, the people attending consider themselves students and usually have a longer-term goal in mind. They also, at least in the best programs, get evaluated on their work and receive professional feedback and grades. Few times, if any, does this ever occur in a professional association conference or seminar.

For all the teaching I have done, I can honestly say that little of it has led to direct client engagement. In fact, I probably have given away more consulting advice to students that I really would have charged for in any other circumstance. What has teaching done for me? First, it gave me tremendous confidence in speaking in front of groups and clients. Second, and probably most important, it has become a reputation builder among my colleagues and potential clients. I have found that on more than one occasion, I have been introduced as the professor at XYZ institution before I was mentioned as a consultant. Given that many inside nonprofits do not see the title "consultant" in positive terms, being "the professor" has probably given me entrée where I would not have that otherwise.

If you are seriously interested in teaching, know that there is a sequence, similar to a sports farm system, where you can build your skills and reputation in your nonprofit related discipline.

To start, consider being a guest speaker for an established academic class. Maybe your specialty is nonprofit direct mail? If you know somebody who is already teaching a class on fundraising, you might offer to do a part of that particular lesson, or be an in-class resource person. For online classes, you might offer to be on a class conference call where you can provide your expertise to the group. By the way, don't expect to be paid for this. Do this as a favor for the instructor. In return you might get a nice box of cookies. Do not expect clients out of this, even from graduate programs where the class might be made up of working nonprofit professionals.

The next level up is your local school district continuing education classes. Many are looking for practical skills that they can package at an accessible price for the general public. Nonprofit skill building is always attractive because so many people are involved with grassroots organizations or community youth and sports groups. Consider this a skill building project for you, too. You will hone your instructional abilities and may make some modest connections in the community or get a referral or two.

With this under your belt, approach your local community college about their interest in first, their community education program (noncredit classes) and eventually there evening academic programs (academic, graded classes). Be aware that anything beyond their community education program will require a Master's degree. Few academic institutions will bring on bachelor only prepared faculty. The community education programs are very similar to the local school district community education programs. Again, this is a way of making some connections getting a little bit of money, and maybe some referrals.

If you have the academic background that a four-year university seeks for an adjunct faculty member, then by all means contact them about continuing education programs at either a bachelors or masters level in nonprofit management. Know that teaching in these programs is in high demand. It might take a while to secure a position. Be persistent if it's a real passion of yours. At some point everybody retires or changes and your name will be top of mind if you have expressed interest and shown a track record of successful instruction.

Exercise 124

Investigate teaching opportunities in your area, or outside your area if you are attracted to teaching online. Make a list of programs, contacts and instructors at:

____ Local school districts

____ Community Centers

____ Community Colleges

____ Four year (+) academic institutions

Webinars

Another iteration of speaking is the webinar. Like the word combination implies, this is a web based seminar. Some consultants, freelancers and vendors will sponsor these themselves, and others will do them as part of a professional association. The advantage of connecting with a professional association is the pool of potential attendees. If you do a webinar independently, you will also need to generate your own audience.

You might think that a webinar and live seminar are similar. They both convey information. They both (usually) use MS PowerPoint slides or something similar. The similarity might end there. Of course, people receiving the webinar information don't have to leave their desk. Neither do you. That means you need to have the technology capabilities to either host or participate in the webinar. You need to become familiar with software platforms, too. These are simply learning curve issues, not major obstacles.

Like any professionals, your target nonprofit audience is busy, so webinars are attractive because they reduce transportation costs and other time wasters. On the other hand, they are also easy to not attend, even though somebody has made a commitment monetarily and on the calendar. Their boss may have just come in the room, or a crisis occurred in their program, or they just got their head into a project and simply forgot about your webinar. So expect erosion on your numbers attending at a higher rate than an in-person presentation.

One major advantage of a webinar is your ability to record the information and either make it available for others at a later date, or edit it down to use for another purpose. If nothing else, post a link to your webinar, or all or a portion of it on your website. Search engine optimization programs for websites love video.

Exercise 125

___ Practice a webinar format by learning the voice recording function of MS PowerPoint or your favorite slide program. Take the slides you developed for your seminar, and record voice overs until you give a smooth presentation.

Exercise 126

___ Name three publications or websites in your discipline who host webinars. Contact one to learn about what topics they prefer and their criteria for inclusion.

_____

_____

_____

Exercise 127

___ Add your recorded webinar to your website.

Writing

Writing is an excellent way of marketing yourself. It establishes you as a (as much as this is an overused term) "thought leader" in your area of expertise. When clients and fellow consultants, freelancers and vendors see your name in a publication, suddenly you are considered an expert in what you do.

There are several options to begin to develop a marketing program to writing. The simplest may be a blog. Just getting your thoughts out electronically in short bursts, on a regular basis, directed to people who you know could use your advice or expertise, is remarkably powerful. I found the key to a blog is to keep it focused around a particular subject, and make sure that it is regularly produced on a schedule that makes sense to your audience. In my opinion, the best blogs are short blogs that people can read very quickly and pick up the important few points and move along with their day. You might schedule them weekly or biweekly. Your audience may not be up for the intensity of a daily update from you (and you may not be up to the intensity of producing one), and if you make it monthly there likely to have forgotten that you even do one once a month.

Notice that I did not say "newsletter." The word "newsletter" has come to mean long and reading intensive. Even by naming your publication and what really may be your blog a "newsletter," a good number of your potential audience will click "delete" because they simply "don't have time." Honestly, you probably don't have time to write something that long, either. Having multiple articles, even if they are not your own, will take time for you to find. If you discover something that you feel very passionate about your clients and audience receiving that's not your own, simply make it a substitute for your blog that month with a link to the material. (Note: I did not say cut and paste that into your blog. That would be plagiarism. However, you can link to another article after an introduction of it. The author of the other piece would probably appreciate the recognition of their work. If you find that s/he does not, pull it down immediately!)

A blog or newsletter is not your only option. Make contact with trade publications in your area of expertise. Many of them are thirsty for writers. Remember, their business model is not journalistic, but advertising sales. You're providing content, especially content that attracts subscribers, and therefore advertisers who want to appeal to their subscribers, can be a win/win for you and the publisher. Don't expect to get paid for providing this kind of content. For you, it is a visibility builder and a way of demonstrating your expertise to your target market. Once published, make sure that you send a link or scan the article to send to all of your clients and potential clients (and yes, even your mother.) Plus, link to it from your own website.

Moving up the scale is book publication. There's nothing that says expertise in the written word as a pile of those words bound together with some heft. Don't think that you need to seek out a major publishing house to have this impact. (Except for the endorsement factor, a traditional publisher relationship is not what used to be. Nearly to a person, anybody I know who has gone this route has found it frustrating and in some cases, costly. Traditional publishers, especially for trade publications, expect the author to carry much of the promotional burden.)

Consider that your best option may be to self-publish. Without getting into too many of the details here, you have a number of options, from working through the process yourself using programs like Amazon's CreateSpace (https://www.createspace.com/), to engaging a person who will do the mechanics of pulling together a book based on your previous writings. (See the reference to Daniel Poynter and Peter Bowerman publications in the endnotes.)

Exercise 128

____ Open a blog on your website.

Exercise 129

Determine your blog's frequency (daily, weekly, bi-weekly, monthly): _____

Exercise 130

Name the first 10 blog posting topics.

_____

_____

_____

_____

_____

_____

_____

_____

_____

_____

Exercise 131

____ Write the first two blog posts.

Direct Response

You may be familiar with direct response marketing but not even know it. Direct response what you might call "junk mail" in your postal mailbox, or when unfamiliar or unsolicited, "spam" in your email box. Despite those characterizations, direct response is among the most powerful tools in marketing toolkit. Here's some important points about direct response:

- Direct response must be consistent. That means you must keep it up over time, which means that it can get expensive in time and money – even if its email (which has the illusion of being cost-free because you avoid postage and paper).

- Direct response requires good messaging. Think of it this way: "Direct" means you send. "Response" means they reply. You need to give your prospects something to reply to. "Awareness" is not a reason to communicate. Always give what's called a "call to action." A call to action is your telling your prospect what you want he or she to do as a result of reading your message. "Call for your free special event evaluation today" is a call to action.

- Direct response can be measured. This is one of the beauties of direct response. In email marketing, programs like MyEmma, Constant Contact, MailChimp and Aweber have sophisticated systems telling you who opened your email, who clicked on an offer and more. While not quite as easy, you can track postal mail marketing through techniques like coding.

- Direct response works best when it is multi-channeled. Direct response works best when you combine it with forms of itself. For example, if you're sending postcards, follow them up with emails. These two forms of direct response are much more likely to produce responses that each on its own.

- Direct response depends upon building a solid database of people who are interested in your services. Better to have a responsive list of 100 clients than a speculative list of 1000 prospects who toss or delete your message the instant they see it.

While all of these (and many more) are important in building a successful direct response program, as someone starting out in consulting, the last point is the most critical. Direct response doesn't work unless you send it to someone. But to whom? That's why building your list is your most important direct response task.

In our culture, paper and email "etiquette" diverge on this point.

The email culture is strongly tilted toward "opt-in." Someone must give their express permission to received your communication. Here's a summary of the US Law called the CANNED SPAM Act that regulates commercial emails:

https://www.ftc.gov/system/files/documents/plain-language/bus61-can-spam-act-compliance-guide-business.pdf.

Canada has similar regulations: http://fightspam.gc.ca/eic/site/030.nsf/eng/home. Any of the above named services will comply, and remind you to comply, with at least the American law.

By the way… why use email services like Constant Contact and the rest? For a number or reasons: They monitor issues like government regulations to guide (force?) you into compliance. Having volumes of mail coming from your personal account will soon get many of your personal emails blocked. They offer good database management. They have templates you can use to develop emails. There's more, too. Check a couple of the services to see.

Warning: "Scraping" is not good. Scraping? Although I doubt whether you will do this in any automated form (which is where the word comes from), scraping is going to websites and gathering names in the contact areas to add to your database so you can send unrequested emails. For example, let's say you offer accounting services to nonprofits. Were you to identify a list of potential client nonprofits, go to each organization's website, and copy/paste their CFO's name and email into your email program, you would be "scraping."

Alternatively, paper/postal mail is much more of an "opt-out" culture. While you may be wasting your time and money sending mail to people who really don't want it, many fewer people get upset about receiving an unsolicited post card or envelope, and easily throw them away (or better yet, recycle them.) Yes, it is possible to hand stuff letters or print post cards from your home printer. If you come from a nonprofit background, you may have extensive experience in organizing "stuffing parties." Yet it is much more efficient (albeit more expensive) to have these functions performed by a printer and/or mail house.

Exercise 132

____ Using a CRM you identified earlier, begin collecting names and addresses of people you think would be receptive to hearing about your service offerings. Expressly ask them for permission to receive mail from you.

Advertising

When most people think "marketing," "advertising" pops up in their mind. Yet for consultants, advertising is probably one of the least effective ways to drive inquiries to your business. I know several well regarded, successful consulting firms and independent consultants who never advertise and do very well. I also know successful firms who advertise, but in my observation, they advertised well after they became successful, as part of a broader branding strategy.

Yes, advertising will get you some "exposure," but to be effective, you need to be out there all of the time, and measuring the results even of long exposure, can be very difficult.

So, why advertise?

It could be that you want to sponsor an event at your local professional association, or put your name into a chamber of commerce directory.

Exercise 133

____ Using MS Word, create a "business card" advertisement for your consultancy that can be easily placed in an event ad book or another local business directory. Make sure to include a "call to action."

Is there a consulting association in your area?

Working with nonprofits as a freelancer or consultant can be a pretty lonely business. There's the working at home or in another office space by yourself. There's doing some of your work at a client's remote location, where you only visit episodically. There's interacting with clients, but not quite being "one of the gang" since you are not employed full-time there. Maybe you're the only consultant you know?

Let's face it, you need to get out and meet some people just like you.

That's why, increasingly, there are associations of nonprofit consultants in many parts of the country. In fact, (a shameless plug here) ThinkNP exists, in part, to connect busy consultants who can't connect in-person.

Get involved in an association of nonprofit consultants. Meeting fellow consultants can certainly help you wade through the issues around isolation. Maybe just as important, you let others know that you're in business, you build you a network for referring business, and you come away with business referrals. Don't think of these people as your competitors. They're your colleagues who can easily supplement your work for your clients, and you can do the same for them.

If an organization doesn't exist, it might be time to start one in your area. The one that I belong to was started by a number of us responding to a call by a colleague to meet at a local coffee shop. Nearly 10 years later, we're still going strong. Many of the faces have changed, and we now meet at a local college's conference room, but the purpose remains the same: to engage each other personally and professionally for our own benefit and that of our clients.

The typical meeting involves introducing each other around the table, particularly focusing on the new people attending. Exchanging business cards, again making sure that the new people feel welcome and that you get their contact information. Sharing the recent successes or information that you have heard in the local nonprofit environment, and asking for help for a particular question that may have come up since last meeting either about business processes or a nonprofit situation. Clients names are usually kept confidential, although you'll find that in smaller communities a few short words will lead to somebody recognizing the nonprofit organization you are discussing.

In addition, many meetings have a program component. You have a number of options here.

1) Somebody among the group addresses a particular business or nonprofit topic, like how to use direct mail in marketing your services.

2) A particular consultant is selected to do an in-depth review of his or her consulting practice. This way, fellow members can better understand how to use this person's talent or refer business to him or her.

3) A nonprofit is to come in for one hour of free consulting with the group. This has been very successful in not only attracting attendees, but allowing group members to see how each other thinks in real-life situations. The nonprofits go away finding that they received value from the experience. Some will even call a consultant they met for further services. However, the ground rules have always stated that the nonprofit would not be directly called by any of the consultants present. The idea was to assure the attending nonprofit that this was legitimate consulting and not a sales oriented shark tank. (Honestly, we revisit this rule sometimes.)

You might also consider seasonal programs, such as a holiday breakfast, or a summer social.

Instead of the above, the "organization" could simply be a group of your best friend consultants gathering for coffee every month or every quarter. The point is that by connecting with fellow consultants, freelancers and vendors, you begin to build a network that you can call upon for professional, or even personal matters.

Exercise 134

____ Look for an association of nonprofit consultants in your area. If there isn't one, consider starting one.

Time to Pick

Now that you have your background marketing information, and you know the tools at your disposal, it's time to pick which ones you're going to use.

Exercise 135

First, let's look at the tactics we discussed above:

- Advertising

- Attending special events

- Conducting special events

- Direct response

- One-to-one networking

- Social media

- Speaking

- Teaching

- Webinars

- Writing

- Association creation

It's important to go with your natural strengths, so name two that are in your "comfort zone." Then, to stretch you a bit, select one method you're not sure about – because you don't feel comfortable with it, or because you don't know that much about the method.

I am comfortable with:

_____

_____

I'll also give this one a try:

_____

Set your objectives:

No, I don't mean numeric goals. We'll get to that, below. I mean "what do I want to get out of doing this particular marketing method?"

If you're familiar with grant proposal writing, you may have run into the "logic model" approach. In short, a logic model has three phases:

- Inputs

- Outputs

- Outcomes

Let's take event attendance as an example marketing method. In attending events, ...

- Your Input could be the money you spend to buy your ticket for an event of 100 people.

- Your Output could be meeting 10 new people at an event of 100 people.

- Your Outcome could be developing a network of personal contacts who refer clients.

So, what's your objective, the ideal Output, you want for the method you selected and the activity you will carry out for that method?

Exercise 136

Name at least one objective for each marketing method you selected:

_____

_____

_____

_____

_____

_____

Now that you selected marketing methods to pursue, you need to lay out a calendar to implement them. This is relatively easy to do in an Excel spreadsheet.

Exercise 137

Step 1: Create your spreadsheet.

Figure 1, marketing spreadsheet example:

Quarter:	First Quarter		
Week:	1	2	3
Marketing Method			
Advertising			
Attending special events			

Figure 1 shows the "X" axis (the top line) divided by four quarters. The "Y" Axis are your selected methods of marketing.

Exercise 138

Step 2: Commit to goals for each marketing method you select. For example, …

For "attending special events" you could set a goal of going to two events each quarter. You might even be more specific, by saying "two events of no less than 100 attendees per quarter"

For advertising, you might say "place one advertisement every month in a publication or website that reaches 2000 subscribers or more."

Exercise 139

Step 3: Next, conduct some research. For example, …

If you already belong to associations that conduct events that meet your "no less than 100 attendees" criteria, then look for the events in their website and schedule the events into your calendar so you can meet your goal.

Exercise 140

Step 4: Insert checkpoints.

Schedule in times to review your plan and make adjustments as necessary. Remember, you run the plan, the plan doesn't need to run you. So if conditions change, or you're not getting what you want out of a certain method, change the plan!

Exercise 141

Step 5: Create and insert "Backdates."

Early in my career I was introduced to "backdating." Backdating is when you set an event or act in your calendar, like a drop date for a mailing or an event date and time. Then you work backwards to create due dates for all of the steps necessary to successfully carry out that project. In a direct mail project, backdated steps could include dates that:

- Copywriting is complete.

- You contact the designer.

- The design is approved.

- And much more.

Exercise 142

Step 6: Work your plan.

Now that you have your plan outlined, put dates into the calendar you use every day to review your plan activities. This should be at least once a month, maybe even once a week.

5 CONCLUSION

I'm sure you've heard the saying for when you make a speech… "Tell 'em what you're going to say. Say it. Then tell 'em what you said." Well, here's what I said:

1) Figure out whether consulting to nonprofits is the right path for you.
2) Build your support systems.
3) Make sure you have the money and legal issues in place.
4) Market and sell, then do it again and again!
5) Work!

(Or, to quote just about every shampoo bottle in the world: "Apply shampoo. Lather. Rinse. Repeat." Except this time, you need to repeat, and repeat, and repeat again.)

Sounds simple, right? Well, it's not overly complicated. What it takes is persistence, with a good dose of self-confidence.

Persistence? Yes. It's easy to get complacent, especially when you're in a time of your consulting business when everyone seems to be coming to you for work, or you're busy with everything else in life. You start rationalizing inattentiveness to your marketing. "It's not money I need to spend this month." Or, "I don't have time." Or, "I'm living on referrals, why do I need to market?" Believe me, it can catch up to you quickly. Panic is not a strategy.

How do you find time for persistence? Put systems in place that "automate your persistence." For example, it could be a simple Google Alert looking for your town name and "nonprofit." When any press release, newspaper article, or mention of that combination comes up, you're the first to know.

Add in a client name (or potential client name), and you look plugged in to everything in your community when you meet that potential client at the next networking event.

Even if you chose to be a part-time consultant, persistence counts. Even if it's just going to professional association events and keeping your ears open for opportunities, or telling your best-work friends that you're open to doing some outside consulting, if you want the extra income, you need to stay "out there" so your potential clients know they can use your services. And if you plan to do this full-time, then it takes a full-time commitment. Half-way doesn't pay the rent.

Self-confident? For sure. Believe me, there are days (and maybe I should only be speaking for myself on this one?) when you'll feel like everyone else is smarter and faster and just plain better than you at doing this "nonprofit consulting thing." That's okay. Walk the dog, visit your mom, eat some chocolate, or do whatever you do to give yourself solace.

Then realize that you're as bright as anyone else out there (and believe me, you are.) I am not suggesting that you are good at everything. I'm not, for sure. Yet while you may not have experience in something, like the intricate details of Excel, for example, it doesn't mean you can't master them. It's really more of a choice. Do you spend the time to get good at Excel, or pay someone else to do the Excel related work while you do something you like and feel more confident in? Whether you outsource or learn it, you build the self-confidence in getting something accomplished. Yes, you can have control in your life, make a dollar, and because you're consulting to nonprofits, make a difference in at least one person's life. It's a win/win.

So, are you ready to go?

Over these many pages we've covered nearly all the essentials of getting you started on consulting with nonprofits. We've discussed why you want to be a consultant, to how to build the structure of your venture, to how to market your services so you can get clients. You've filled out blank lines and checked boxes while thinking about the nuances of your business. You've reached out to friends, family and professional services for support.

Still, as much as I hope you enjoyed this book, or better yet, are able to put what you read and saw immediately to work, reading this book is not going to make you a consultant.

What will?

Doing it.

Don't be disappointed if your first jobs are not your ideal jobs. I have an attorney friend who tells me that her first work in independent practice was collecting bad debts for dentists. She was a dental hygienist at the start of her work-life, and knew enough about dental practices that dentists trusted her. It got her started, and she soon moved to jobs that she found much more interesting and suited her personality better. Who knows, maybe you'll start by writing grant proposals for start-ups, then move to what you really love, running capital campaigns? Or maybe you'll get a few nonprofits who like your design work, then transition to what really charges you up: advising them on marketing.

So that makes my last point maybe the most important point: be flexible. Sometimes quickly sometimes not, your "market," (however you label it, from hospitals needing accounting to nature centers needing fundraising) will tell you what you are good at and how they can use your talents. You just have to listen to them, and yourself. Listen to yourself is finding what energizes you in how you serve your clients. If you really liked teaching their board how to function as a team, maybe you should focus on that and leave fundraising behind. Conversely, listen to others, especially your clients. If you get rave reviews about what you thought was an "anybody can do this" board training session, maybe not everyone can do it? Many times other people see what you're good at before you do. If you get consistent pushback on something you do all of the time, maybe it's time to shift to work that's less frustrating for the client, and you.

Either way, it took some time after I "officially" started before I was able to tell anyone that I was a consultant. Maybe I didn't believe it? With each client I grew into the role. With each job I saw that I was able to offer greater and greater benefit to those I served… or more importantly, who they served. Maybe that's what the difference is in working with nonprofits? Yes, you are serving your clients. But like the nonprofit, you are ultimately serving their clients, even if you never directly touch them.

Best of luck in your path. It is uniquely your own. I hope that ThinkNP can be there to light the way to your success.

Matt Hugg
Lansdale, Pennsylvania, USA

6 BOOKS, ORGANIZATIONS, SOFTWARE/HARDWARE AND WEBSITES

Books

- **Bowerman, Peter:** Several titles at https://www.amazon.com/Peter-Bowerman/e/B001JS4SPK

- Duckworth, Angela: **Grit: The Power of Passion and Perseverance** (Scribner, 2016) ISBN-13: 978-1501111112

- Fox, Jeffrey J.: **How to make big money in your own small business: unexpected rules every small business owner needs to know** (2004 Hyperion, New York, New York) ISBN-13: 978-0786868254

- Tracy Gary, Suze Orman (Foreword by) with Nancy Adess: **Inspired Philanthropy: Your Step-by-Step Guide to Creating a Giving Plan and Leaving a Legacy**, 3rd Edition, ISBN: 978-0-7879-9652-9

- Gerber, Michael: **The E-Myth Revisited**: Why Most Small Businesses Don't Work and What to Do About It (HarperCollins, 1995) ISBN: 978-0887307287

- Honeyman, Ryan: **The B Corp Handbook**: How to Use Business as a Force for Good (Berrett-Koehler Publishers, 2014) ISBN: 978-1626560437

- Judson, Bruce: **Go It Alone!** The Secret to Starting a Successful Business on Your Own (Harper Business, 2004) ISBN 0-06-073113-3

- Mancuso, Anthony: LLC or Corporation? **How to Choose the Right Form for Your Business**, 6th Ed. (Nolo, 2014) ISBN: 978-1413320749

- **Poynter, Daniel**: several titles at
  https://www.amazon.com/Dan-Poynter/e/B000AQTRJE/

- Reis, Eric: **The Lean Startup:** How Today's Entrepreneurs Use Continuous Innovation to Create Radically Successful Businesses (Crown Business, 2010) ISBN: 978-0307887894

- RoAne, Susan: **How to Work a Room**, 25th Anniversary Edition: The Ultimate Guide to Making Lasting Connections--In Person and Online (William Morrow Paperbacks, 2014) ISBN: 0062295349

- Schiffman, Stephen: **Cold Calling Techniques** (That Really Work!), 7th ed. (Adams Media, 2014) ISBN: 978-1440572173

- Teegarden, Paige Hull; Hinden, Denice Rothman; Teegarden, Paul Sturm: **The Nonprofit Organizational Culture Guide**: Revealing the Hidden Truths that Impact Performance (Jossey-Bass, 2010) ISBN: 978-0470891544

Organizations

- **Association of Fundraising Professionals:** www.afpnet.org

- **B Lab**: www.bcorporation.net

- **Elks**: www.elks.org

- **Free and Accepted Masons**: www.msana.com/linksus.asp

- **Kiwanis International**: www.kiwanis.org

- **National Speakers Association**: www.nsaspeaker.org

- **Rotary**: www.rotary.org

- **SCORE** (Service Corps of Retired Executives): www.score.org

- **Small Business Administration (SBA) Centers**:
  www.sba.gov/tools/local-assistance/sbdc

- **The National Council of Nonprofit Associations:** www.ncna.org

- **Toastmasters:** www.toastmasters.org

Software/Hardware

- Accounting

  o **Quicken:** www.quicken.com

  o **QuickBooks**: quickbooks.intuit.com

  o **Freshbooks:** www.freshbooks.com

- Book development

  o **CreateSpace**: www.createspace.com

- Cloud Storage

  o **Microsoft OneDrive:** onedrive.live.com

  o **Google Drive**: www.google.com/drive

  o **DropBox**: hwww.dropbox.com

  o **Box**: www.box.com

  o **Amazon's Cloud**: www.amazon.com/clouddrive

- CRMs

  o **Insightly**: www.insightly.com

  o **Zoho**: https: www.zoho.com

- Hardware:

  o **Chromebook**: www.google.com/chromebook

- Notebooks

  o **Evernote**: www.evernote.com

  o **Microsoft OneNote**: www.onenote.com

- Office Utilities

  o **Apache OpenOffice**: https://www.openoffice.org/

- o **Gmail**: https://mail.google.com/

- o **Microsoft Outlook**: https://www.microsoft.com/en-us/outlook-com/

- Security

  - o **Norton**: us.norton.com

  - o **McAfee**: www.mcafee.com

- Social Media

  - o **Facebook**: www.facebook.com

  - o **LinkedIn**: www.linkedin.com

  - o **Meetup**: www.meetup.com

  - o **Twitter**: twitter.com

- Web Hosts

  - o **1and1**: www.1and1.com

  - o **GoDaddy**: www.godaddy.com

  - o **HostGator**: www.hostgator.com

Websites

- Articles

  - o **American commuting times**
    http://www.usatoday.com/story/news/nation/2013/03/05/americans-commutes-not-getting-longer/1963409/

  - o **Business Survival Rates**
    https://www.linkedin.com/pulse/20140915223641-170128193-what-are-the-real-small-business-survival-rates

- o **The man who would be King (of America)**
  http://www.newsweek.com/americas-lost-monarchy-man-who-would-be-king-92243

- ● Legal References

  - o **American Bar Association Directory**:
    apps.americanbar.org/legalservices/lris/directory/

  - o **American Bar Association**:
    apps.americanbar.org/legalservices/findlegalhelp/home.cfm

  - o **Canada's Anti-Spam Legislation**:
    http://fightspam.gc.ca/eic/site/030.nsf/eng/home

  - o **CANNED SPAM Act:**
    https://www.ftc.gov/system/files/documents/plain-language/bus61-can-spam-act-compliance-guide-business.pdf

  - o **GivingUSA Annual Survey of State Laws Regulating Charitable Solicitations**:
    http://givingusa.org/product/giving-usa-2015-spotlight-annual-survey-of-state-laws-regulating-charitable-solicitations-as-of-january-1-2015/

  - o **Martindale Hubbell Find Lawyers**:
    www.martindale.com/Find-Lawyers-and-Law-Firms.aspx

  - o **Nolo, Law Firms & Lawyers**: www.nolo.com/lawyers

- ● Financial Resources

  - o **Internal Revenue Service (IRS)** on Enrolled Agents:
    https://www.irs.gov/tax-professionals/enrolled-agents/enrolled-agent-information

  - o **Internal Revenue Service (IRS),** W-9 Form:
    https://www.irs.gov/pub/irs-pdf/fw9.pdf

  - o **National Association of Tax Preparers**, Entity Comparison:
    http://www.natptax.com/TaxKnowledgeCenter/FederalTaxInformation/Documents/Chart%20of%20Entity%20Comparison.pdf

- o **SCORE** on Start Up Expenses
  https://www.score.org/resource/start-expenses

- Email Marketing Programs

  - o Aweber: **https://www.aweber.com/**

  - o Constant Contact: **https://www.constantcontact.com/**

  - o MailChimp: **https://mailchimp.com/**

  - o MyEmma: http://myemma.com/

- Other Sites

  - o **Habitat for Humanity's Re-Stores**: www.habitat.org/restores

  - o **Microsoft Suite templates**: templates.office.com

  - o **Myers-Briggs**: www.mbtionline.com

7 EXERCISE CHECKLIST

Check them off as you complete them.

__ Exercise 1	__ Exercise 29
__ Exercise 2	__ Exercise 30
__ Exercise 3	__ Exercise 31
__ Exercise 4	__ Exercise 32
__ Exercise 5	__ Exercise 33
__ Exercise 6	__ Exercise 34
__ Exercise 7	__ Exercise 35
__ Exercise 8	__ Exercise 36
__ Exercise 9	__ Exercise 37
__ Exercise 10	__ Exercise 38
__ Exercise 11	__ Exercise 39
__ Exercise 12	__ Exercise 40
__ Exercise 13	__ Exercise 41
__ Exercise 14	__ Exercise 42
__ Exercise 15	__ Exercise 43
__ Exercise 16	__ Exercise 44
__ Exercise 17	__ Exercise 45
__ Exercise 18	__ Exercise 46
__ Exercise 19	__ Exercise 47
__ Exercise 20	__ Exercise 48
__ Exercise 21	__ Exercise 49
__ Exercise 22	__ Exercise 50
__ Exercise 23	__ Exercise 51
__ Exercise 24	__ Exercise 52
__ Exercise 25	__ Exercise 53
__ Exercise 26	__ Exercise 54
__ Exercise 27	__ Exercise 55
__ Exercise 28	__ Exercise 56

INDEX

ABOUT THE AUTHOR

Matt Hugg is a nonprofit consultant and president of ThinkNP.com, an online educational resource for consultants, freelancers and vendors to nonprofit organizations.

Over his 30-year career he's held fundraising leadership positions at the Boy Scouts of America, Lebanon Valley College, the University of Cincinnati, Ursinus College and the University of the Arts. Matt teaches fundraising, philanthropy and marketing in graduate programs at Juniata College, Eastern University, the University of Pennsylvania and Thomas Edison State College. He holds a bachelor's degree from Juniata College in Huntingdon, Pennsylvania and a master's in Philanthropy and Development from St. Mary's University of Minnesota.

See Matt's (and other's) videos, podcasts and articles on how to build your business serving nonprofits at ThinkNP.com